Growing Together

Dr David Fontana has more than twenty-five years' experience in child psychology and the study of spiritual growth. He is a fellow of the British Psychological Society and Reader in Educational Psychology at the University of Wales, Cardiff. He is the author of fifteen different books on psychology and personal development which have been translated over forty times into all major world and European languages.

selected titles by the same author

DREAMLIFE
THE ELEMENTS OF MEDITATION
THE MEDITATOR'S HANDBOOK
YOUR GROWING CHILD: FROM BIRTH TO ADOLESCENCE
THE EDUCATION OF THE YOUNG CHILD
THE SECRET LANGUAGE OF SYMBOLS
THE SECRET LANGUAGE OF DREAMS

Growing Together

PARENT-CHILD RELATIONSHIPS
AS A PATH
TO WHOLENESS AND HAPPINESS

David Fontana

ELEMENT
Shaftesbury, Dorset • Rockport, Massachusetts
Brisbane, Queensland

Published in Great Britain in 1994 by
Element Books Ltd
Shaftesbury, Dorset

Published in the USA in 1994 by
Element, Inc.
42 Broadway, Rockport, MA 01966

Published in Australia in 1994 by
Element Books Ltd
for Jacaranda Wiley Ltd
33 Park Road, Milton, Brisbane, 4064

Cover illustrations:
Mother and Child by TCL Stock Directory UK
Family Picnic by Stockphotos, Inc.
Father and Daughter by Stockphotos, Inc.
Grandfather & Granddaughter by Telegraph Colour Library
Cover design by Peter Bridgewater Books
Page design by Roger Lightfoot
Typeset by ROM-Data Corporation, Falmouth, Cornwall
Printed and bound in Great Britain by Redwood Books,
Trowbridge, Wiltshire

British Library Cataloguing in Publication
data available

Library of Congress Cataloging in Publication
data available

ISBN 1-85230-559-2

Contents

Introduction vi

1. Preparing for Parenthood 1
2. The Child's World 20
3. Learning and Growing: I 31
4. Learning and Growing: II 46
5. The Child as Scientist 67
6. The Child as Artist and Problem-Solver 80
7. The Child and God 91
8. Magic, Terrors and Dreaming 109
9. The Child at School 123
10. Body and Mind 138

Conclusion 148

Further Reading 150

Useful Addresses 151

Index 152

Introduction

This book is about being a parent in what are, by general agreement, particularly challenging times. Many of the old social guidelines and constraints are breaking down. Children are exposed as never before to undesirable role models on television and in the media generally. Organized religion appears to answer the needs of fewer and fewer people. Violence and lawlessness are increasing. The world at large is a very unsafe place. Yet parents still receive virtually no help at being parents. Though parenting is arguably the most important job any of us do, it is a job for which no formal training of any consequence is offered. Parents have to learn as best they can by talking to friends, by remembering the good and bad examples of their own parents, and (often with disastrous consequences) by a process of trial and error.

Yet although not always easy to put into effect, good parenting, wise parenting, consists of following a relatively few, reasonably flexible guidelines, and doing so with love and consistency. This book attempts to set out these guidelines. It is based throughout upon sound modern psychological and educational research, but it aims to present these guidelines in a straightforward, informal, and above all practical way. Most parents need neither to be lectured at nor to be dazzled by science. Their most pressing need is to be helped to know what to *do*.

Although the book is aimed at all parents, it has particularly in mind those who take a deep interest in life, who are concerned for the environment, who have a sense that there may be spiritual realities underlying the world of appearances, who take an interest in their children as budding scientists and artists, who want to give them a life of the mind as well as of the body, and who aim to enjoy with them the few precious years it takes for the new baby to grow into the mature man or woman. Such parents care about their children in a very particular way, and the bonds they form with them are immensely strong yet at the same time non-restrictive. They are the bonds of a love that cherishes without stifling, that guides without coercing, that knows and values the balance between freedom and responsibility, and that wants above all that children find fulfillment and meaning in life.

Parental circumstances differ widely of course, and no single book can hope to cover them all. This book therefore takes as most typical the two-parent family of mother and father, but most of the information given can be adapted to suit individual situations. The basic needs of the child do not change just because those of the parents do. This is not for one moment to minimize the extra demands that are made upon single parents, or the emotionally difficult demands often made of step-parents. Life is very much harder for some parents (and thus for some children) than for others. This book aims simply to set out what we know about the framework of good parenting, and to invite individuals, within this framework, to proceed in accordance with the constraints and the opportunities of their particular set of circumstances.

One last point. If we are honest we have to admit that however hard we try we none of us do as well as we would like in any of the important areas of life. We have an ideal, and we usually fall short of that ideal. This is part of being human, and we shouldn't feel too badly about ourselves in consequence. But unless we have an ideal, we have nothing against which to measure our present performance. In parenting perhaps more than in anything else we need this ideal.

Enjoy your children!

CHAPTER 1

Preparing for Parenthood

The poet William Wordsworth in his 'Intimations of Immortality from Recollections of Early Childhood' writes that:

> Our birth is but a sleep and a forgetting:
> The Soul that rises with us, our life's Star,
> Hath had elsewhere its setting,
> And cometh from afar:
> Not in entire forgetfulness,
> And not in utter nakedness,
> But trailing clouds of glory do we come
> From God, who is our home:
> Heaven lies about us in our infancy!

'Trailing clouds of glory do we come'. What a sublime metaphor, and what a reminder that there are two ways of looking at the new-born baby. One is to see it as a helpless new life, fresh from the womb and bringing nothing to the world except its genetic inheritance from its parents. A new life, with everything to learn, and not unlike the first blank page in an exercise book on which experience waits to write its messages. The other is to see it as an entry (perhaps a re-entry) into the world of a life that stretches back into an unknown and unimaginable past. A continuation of an immortal existence that brings as much into the world as it will across the years take from it.

Which of these views we prefer – and I shall return to the issues concerned as the book unfolds – is very much a matter of personal choice. But there is no doubt that the choice we make profoundly affects our view of infancy, and influences not only our attitudes and behaviour towards the child but also the way in which we interpret his or her every action. Some parents, even without having made their choice consciously, will say of a new-born child that he or she has been here before. What they mean by this is that there is a quality of knowing about the child, a sense that, without being able to express him- or herself in words, the child brings with it a store of wisdom, and looks out at the world not with incomprehension but with a form of recognition.

This view of childhood grants us a special respect for the new-born. We see the baby as already possessing his or her own personality, as having a certain independence and power of self-determination, as not belonging to us, in the sense of being our personal property. Moreover, we see the baby as having much to teach us, as a master or mistress of wisdom and not just as a pupil in the first days at a new school. Some parents take matters further, and see the child as having chosen to come into the world in order to develop further, and indeed as having chosen to be born to them rather than to anyone else. The child has voluntarily entrusted him- or herself to them, and the trust is a very precious and sacred one.

Even for parents who take the alternative view, and see the child as newly made, the thrill of creating a life where none existed before carries with it its own sense of wonder and gratitude. Whatever our views on its origins and purpose, we cannot help but stand in awe before the magic of creation, and cannot fail to recognize the beauty of the gift that nature has bestowed upon us.

WE ALSO ARE PART OF NATURE

In recognizing this gift, we must allow ourselves to acknowledge an even deeper truth, namely that 'nature' includes ourselves. Language tricks us easily into thinking of nature as some abstract force 'out there', instead of a living process of which we are as much a part as the wind and the rain and the brilliance of sunlight. The ancients believed that nature was a seamless garment, or a vast web in which everything was interconnected, and the truth of this view of reality is not difficult to grasp. The food we eat, the air we breathe, come directly from the outside world and return in due course to it. The water, the calcium, the copper, the iron, and the range of other materials of which our bodies are composed are identical with the water, calcium and so on in the rest of nature. Even the very atoms of our bodies are identical with the atoms outside. Life flows into and through and around us in a perpetual dance of being. We are the shapes, the configurations, that this dance takes, just as water vapour takes the form of clouds and sunlight takes the form of light and shadow.

Hindu philosophy, which understands these things at a profounder level than much of Western thought, speaks of life, nature, reality, as the dance of the god Siva, a constant arising, forming, passing away, and re-arising; it speaks of it as *leela*, as the playfulness of eternity. And not only are our bodies part of this dance but so also are our thoughts and our actions. Buddhism talks of 'dependent origination', the never-ending chain of circumstances upon which everything depends and into which everything is woven. The objects, events and ideas that make up our lives have innumerable causes stretching back into beginningless time. Demonstrate it to yourself by asking a simple question such as 'what causes my car?' The answer is not just the driver and the technicians who designed and built the engine, but an endless succession of other factors such as the workers who dug the iron ore that is its raw material, the iron ore itself, the organic life that yielded the petrol or diesel in its tank, and so on right back to whatever created the material world in the first place. Equally, the 'cause' of our own individual existence on earth is not just our parents but the long chain of our ancestors stretching back to the beginnings of organic life. Even our thoughts themselves are the result not just of our own consciousness but of the combined consciousness of the same innumerable forebears.

The new-born baby is also a consequence of this ceaseless play and inter-play of life, indeed in a real sense a very special symbol of it because it is formed by the union of male and female, the twin forces of creation and of the energies inside ourselves that must flow in harmony if we are to experience psychological wholeness. These forces are well represented in the tai-chi (or yin-yang) symbol of the Chinese Taoists, which when set in motion combines its separate shapes and colours into a dynamic unity. We see it also in the symbolic language of the medieval alchemists, who spoke of turning base metal into gold by means of the chemical wedding of the red king and the white queen, and we see it again in the Egyptian ank, which combines the masculine three-pointed cross with the feminine oval to form one of the most beautiful of all symbols of union and of eternal perfection.

These and allied issues will be returned to in their proper place later in the book, but they remind us right at the outset that at the moment of conception the male and female forces in the universe combine to provide a vehicle through which life expresses itself anew. In the moment of conception, male and female represent the creative force in the universe, in no way separate from that creative energy that brings into being all life.

THE MEANING OF WISE PARENTHOOD

In this sense, the moment of conception is a sacred ritual in that it is dedicated, consciously or unconsciously, to creation itself. And from conception onwards the sacred ritual becomes a sacred responsibility. Having provided for the entry of life into the world, male and female each carry a duty to provide it with the conditions under which it can grow and fulfil the potential it brings with it. These conditions include the love and care and other gifts that provide much of the subject matter of this book, but they also include a recognition of the gift of grace that the young child in turn brings with it. Without an acknowledgement and constant remembrance of this gift, both mother and father risk failing to honour their child in the way that he or she deserves, and failing to experience to the full the joy that parenthood can give.

Ultimately, joy is the parental birthright. No one can pretend that parenthood is always easy, or that it doesn't bring its times of anxiety, discord, and physical and mental exhaustion. But of all the tasks that men and women can undertake in life, parenthood is perhaps the most fruitful and rewarding. Speak to any parents who have borne their first child only after many years of longing and trying, and who appreciate to the full the blessing that has at last come into their lives. The yearning for a child exists in most of us, no matter how deeply it may be hidden, and when this yearning has to wait many years to be satisfied, the mind and the heart are in a fit state to appreciate and cherish the moment of fulfilment.

Enlightened parenting, the subject of this book, is about this joy, about the recognition of a sacred responsibility, and about providing the conditions under which the child can grow and fulfil a potential that embraces intellectual, emotional, social and spiritual development, and that covers the creative, imaginative inner life as well as relationships with the outer world. Enlightened parenting is an acknowledgement in the child of all those things that make us truly human, and that enhance the lives of self and of others. It is about studying the child and learning who he or she really is, instead of dwelling on our own demands and on artificial expectations as to who we think the child ought to be. It is in truth an acknowledgement of the mystery, complexity and beauty of life itself.

THE TIME BEFORE BIRTH

An absence of expectations does not mean that in the months between conception and delivery it is wrong to have dreams of whom the child may become in the years that lie ahead; but it is important always to see these dreams for what they are, the product of our own creative, delightful, playful imagination. At times we may believe that it is our unborn child who is whispering these dreams to us in those quiet moments when the mind withdraws from the outer world and listens to itself, but we must beware of building them into certainties. Our child must be him- or herself. The greatest search a child will make in life is for identity, and this search is immeasurably harder if the demands and the restrictions placed upon him or her by adults control too tightly the formative early years. 'Who am I?' the child will ask, and we must ensure that in the years ahead the answer will be forthcoming from him or herself.

If it is not, then in its place there will be only inadequacy and loss. The child will not have learned the sense of self-worth and self-esteem that brings with it the assurance that we each have a right to self-acceptance and to our own space in the world. When working with troubled or depressed adults I find, like many psychologists and psychiatrists, that the problem almost always comes back to this inability to value oneself. However successful the individuals concerned may now be in their professional lives, however wealthy or bright with honours, they are still prevented by the way they were conditioned in childhood from seeing themselves as authentic and worthwhile human beings.

In the months before birth it is vital therefore not to sketch out in our minds a ready-made identity for our unborn child. Every child must discover and express identity in his or her own way, and be valued for it. Only through being thus valued can self-value arise. This issue will be returned to at greater length in due course, but so vital is it to holistic parenting that it cannot be emphasized too often. In the time before birth it is better therefore to replace expectations about the nature of our unborn child with a sense of curiosity – 'I wonder what he or she will be like?' – 'I look forward with love to our meeting', and to rest in the certainty that the child will be looking forward to it every bit as much.

This sense of wonder, of anticipation, of excitement is enhanced by the use of simple ritual. Such rituals surround child-bearing and childbirth in all cultures; I am talking not about primitive superstitions but about a series of practices that help prepare the minds of both mother and father for the events that lie ahead. In parts of China, it is still traditional for the mother during the months of pregnancy to make a baby sling out of red material (considered a lucky colour), and to decorate it with flowers and with the Chinese pictograms for long life and good fortune. This not only helps her to surround her unborn child with loving and peaceful thoughts but it also is believed to protect the baby from harm after the birth. In rural areas throughout Europe, the father would traditionally make a cradle in readiness for the birth, using oak (sacred to the earth goddess), rowan (believed to give protection against witches and evil spirits), and ash (sacred to the sky god). Sometimes the father-to-be would search the woods for days on end before he was satisfied he had found pieces of wood that had exactly the right feel about them.

This habit of making things in readiness for the child was the result not just of necessity (even among the poor it was always possible to barter for what was wanted), but of the belief that in making something one was endowing it mystically with part of oneself. This is not as fanciful as it seems. Even in modern Japan the master bowmaker or swordsmith prepares himself through meditation for his task, and is said to endow the weapon with his own ki or energy to such an extent that it seems to have a life of its own. And in the West the most prized musical instruments (such as the Stradivarius violin) are claimed by great musicians to have a beauty of sound that can only be attributed in some indefinable way to the spirit of their maker.

It is sad that nowadays, in preparing for a baby, we most of us think no further than the local shops, and surround the young child with dead machine-made objects of chrome and plastic and chipboard, when in reality as much as possible of the baby's world should be hand-made. Hand-made not as a duty but as a way of creating a very special environment of love and care that reflects in the outer world the inner love and care that lay behind the baby's conception. And while creating this world, the mind of the maker should be focused upon the act of creation itself, thus making of each task a form of active meditation. As with all meditation, intrusive thoughts should be ignored, and the mind kept open and clear, and concentrated lightly, almost playfully, and without hurry or irritation upon the task that lies under one's hands. As a result, just as food tastes different when prepared in tranquillity and love, so the baby's room will come to be charged with a special gentle energy.

Singing should also be part of the ritual. The ancients believed that song was a form of magic, because in their wisdom they recognized the power it has to raise consciousness and enthuse the body. It is no accident that singing and chanting are central to the practices of the world's great religions. The Celts regarded singing as a protection against the wiles of the little people, and held that the magician and the wise woman could cast spells through song. The combination of singing, meditation and the use of the hands is particularly powerful, not only in preparing the minds of parents but also, as the unborn child is created from their life force and shares a blood stream with its mother, in preparing the child for the moment of entry into the outer world.

The right frame of mind in both father and mother during pregnancy produces therefore very real physical and psychological benefits for the baby, and helps ensure that he or she will be untroubled in turn during the first months after birth. There is evidence that a mother's negative or anxious attitudes during pregnancy can affect the baby for at least six months after it comes into the world. The adrenalin, nor-adrenalin and other hormones released into the mother's bloodstream in response to her stressed state of mind are shared with the baby during pregnancy, and can leave a residue of fretfulness and nerviness in the latter which persists during these early months. This places a strain upon both parents which in turn affects their relationship with the child and can affect his or her future development.

There are many other rituals that can be used during pregnancy. These must not become compulsive on the one hand or mechanical on the other, but should be done with the express purpose of elevating consciousness and inducing respect and reverence for nature and for the place of parents and child within it. The form of the ritual is of less importance than that it is carried out in the right frame of mind. It is perfectly possible to invent rituals of one's own. Blessing the baby's room each morning and evening is a good example. A prayer can be used from whatever religion parents follow, or a special one can be composed asking that the room be made a fit place to receive the child, that the atmosphere be safe and welcoming, and that the child will receive there the gifts of grace that will help build a happy and useful life. This act of blessing can be accompanied by simple hand gestures, such as the sign of the cross or the sprinkling of holy water or rose water. Sweet smelling incense can be waved towards each corner of the room, or rose petals or the leaves of a sacred herb such as rosemary or lavender strewn on the floor. A crystal can be held up to the window so that it catches the light and scatters rainbows on the walls.

The success of any ritual depends upon the strength of the belief system involved and the level of concentration and emotional involvement that goes into it. At first there may be a feeling of self-consciousness, but if the ritual is practised regularly and in a relaxed frame of mind, it will quickly come to have a powerful meaning, and take its place as a welcome and valuable part of the day.

MIXED EMOTIONS IN THE WAITING MONTHS

Up to now most of what I have said refers to the positive side of the months before birth. But there can be a negative side too. Apart from physical problems, which should be taken care of by appropriate medical treatment, there can be ambivalent feelings, often arising unbidden and unexpectedly, about the prospect of parenthood. During most pregnancies there are occasions when one or both parents starts to doubt their readiness or their suitability for what lies ahead. Will they be able to cope with a child? How much of their present way of life will be forfeit? Will the child be in full physical and mental health? Will – and these can be the most disturbing thoughts of all – one be capable of loving him or her? What if one feels only indifference, or worse still resentment and outright rejection?

These feelings must be seen as natural and temporary. Natural because certainly a major change is about to take place in life. Much will have to be sacrificed as gifts to the coming child. If this is the first experience of parenthood, it is natural also to feel uncertain about one's own capacity for giving the love and care that is needed, and the patience and the time and the guidance. And it is equally natural to have worries about the child's health, and also about the future. How will he or she turn out as they grow into adolescence and adulthood? How will they do at school? Will they be popular with other children? And so on and so on.

If these anxieties are absent, then there is sometimes a suspicion that parents are being unrealistic and perhaps idealistic about what they are taking on. Small babies and young children cannot all the time resemble the sanitized pictures one sees in magazines. They can be awkward, troublesome, obstinate, and all the other things that make parenting at times frustrating and worrying. But to recognize these things now is to help the mind adapt in advance, and to be aware of what the future holds. And this is why such anxieties are temporary as well as natural. As one faces up to them and accepts them, they are seen as simply a part of the process. Whatever gifts we are given by nature, we are asked to give something in return. Our talents require hard work and dedication if they are to be developed. Our relationship with a loved one requires compromise and understanding. Our rose garden requires watering and weeding. Our bodies require care and exercise. The list is endless. Nature, in her wisdom, has decreed that our personal growth and development must depend in large measure upon our readiness to play our own part. She gives her gifts lavishly and lovingly, but she knows that if all we do is hold out our hands and receive them, we will make poor use of them. So she gives us a further gift, the need to bring effort and energy into our lives, and to take some responsibility for what we do and for who we are.

MOTHER–FATHER RELATIONSHIPS IN THE WAITING MONTHS

The rituals I described earlier take on an extra dimension when they are performed by both parents together. They can also bring the future father and mother closer to each other. However, sometimes one parent may take these preparations for the baby seriously, while the other may not. Where this happens and no compromise can be reached, each parent must agree to respect the other's point of view, and carry on in his or her own way. Heated disputes between parents over any aspect of the psycho-spiritual life are best avoided. Neither parent is likely to convince the other through words and argument, and the wisest course is to allow the value of a particular spiritual path to emerge of its own.

For both parents though, there may be worries as to the extent to which their own relationship will be changed by the arrival of a baby. Men sometimes report feelings of jealousy, not only for the attention their partner receives during pregnancy but also for the extent to which her thoughts from now on will be increasingly centred upon the child. They question whether this means that after the birth the child will take their place in her affections.

Women, by contrast, sometimes report anxieties as to whether they will lose their physical attractiveness for a partner once so much of their attention will be taken up by a baby, and that he will in consequence turn towards other women. Both sets of worries are understandable enough, and both are best helped by frank discussion in which doubts are expressed and faced, and reassurances given.

But explicit in these reassurances must be a recognition that the relationship between partners cannot stay the same once a child arrives. One of the main teachings of the great spiritual traditions is that we must accept the reality of change. Change is as inevitable as the cycle of the seasons. We inhabit a dynamic universe within which change and growth are features of all living systems. To attempt to cling on to the past, to try to keep things as they once were, is to condemn ourselves inevitably to disappointment and suffering. Nothing stays the same, and we can either accept this with joy as part of the infinite variety and creativity that characterizes life, or we can waste time in fruitless and misplaced regrets.

The important thing is for partners to discuss in advance the kind of changes that will come into their lives once a baby arrives. At one level this involves practicalities such as how the home will be run and how the extra work will be divided up between the partners. Failure to agree on this division will lead inevitably to friction later on. I met recently the case of a young mother who for 6 months after the birth of her baby never had more than a few hours of broken sleep each night. Not once during this time did her husband get out of bed to attend to the baby in order to allow her to take much needed rest. Not surprisingly, after 6 months she ended up in the local psychiatric hospital. Frequently I am consulted by mothers who tell me that their partners leave them in no doubt that the child is theirs and therefore their responsibility – their 'baggage', as one husband in all seriousness put it.

Clearly this is no basis for a happy relationship. A child is a joint gift and a joint responsibility. Failure by the father to accept this responsibility, and to recognize all it entails, is a failure of his manhood and not an assertion of it. My usual advice to parents is that during the months before birth they draw up a list of the routine household tasks that will need to be done after the baby arrives, and agree on how to allocate them. If one partner is out at work and the other at home, this will influence the form that the division takes, but the division must remain fair to both parties, and must cover not just the daytime but also the nights and the very early mornings. If it proves difficult to agree in certain areas, a perceptive and impartial friend can be asked to arbitrate. This makes it all sound like a contract, but this is exactly what any partnership in a sense is, and there are times when the terms of this contract must be spelled out in proper detail.

At another level, discussion is needed on the emotional side of the new life ahead. In what way will love for a child diminish or add to the love that a man and a woman have for each other? Is love a finite emotion, so that a person has only so much of it to go round, and giving children their fair share means depriving a partner of his or hers? Or does love give rise to more love, so that loving a child strengthens the love for a partner? What are the specific things that may make a man feel jealous of his partner's love for a new baby, and how can these best be handled? What are the things that will help a woman to feel she still remains attractive to her partner, and how can such things be given? By talking these and allied issues through, both partners become clearer on how their emotional place in the life of the other can be safeguarded and enhanced as a child enters their world.

At a further level, thought is needed on how the parents will each relate to the child. There will be agreement between them on the need to give love and care, but what do love and care mean in practical terms? And over and above love and care, how will the child be guided in his or her behaviour, and helped to learn the rules of social living? What in any case are these rules, and how important is each of them? And so on. The issues involved will be returned to again at appropriate points later in the book, but it is no use waiting until the child arrives and then trying to play everything by ear. It is a regrettable fact that parents receive no formal education for their role, and this means that they have much work to do to clarify that role for themselves. Central to it are four ground-rules that must underpin the various detailed decisions that have to be taken. The first of these is that:

1. There should be consistency between parents in how they relate to the child.

Nothing is more confusing for a young mind than to be treated radically differently by each parent (or treated differently by the same parent from one day to the next). To understand the world and his or her place in it, the young child needs to be offered a stable model of how that world works, and of the duties constraints and freedoms that it offers.

The second ground-rule is that:

2. At all times the child should feel secure in the gift of parental love.

This is the most important ground-rule of all, and will be re-emphasized at various times throughout the book. No matter what the disagreements that arise between parents and child, the latter should be confident always that love is not an optional extra, to be withdrawn on the whim of parental displeasure. The love of both parents is the rock that children need if they are to be given a firm foundation to their lives during the vital formative early years. This love must under no circumstances be negotiable, and parents must never by word or deed give the impression that it is.

If the child can also be sure that the love between parents is equally secure, so much the better, but relationships as I said earlier change, and this may not always be possible. But the third ground-rule is that:

3. At the very least, parents should not indulge their anger or hostility towards each other in front of the child.

If the relationship between parents is an unhappy one, then the child will need to know this in due course, but this knowledge must come later, when he or she is mature enough to understand and accommodate to it, and it must come gradually, through explanation and supportive discussion and not through the trauma of watching and hearing parents tear each other apart.

The fourth ground-rule is that:

4. The child should not be expected to provide the emotional support that the parents should ideally be receiving from each other.

This again will be re-emphasized where necessary throughout the book. If the relationship between parents is an unhappy one (or if the child is brought up by a single parent), there is often a strong temptation to turn to the child for the love, the understanding and the support that should come from another adult. This places the child in a role that he or she cannot be expected to sustain, and can cause in him or her extreme feelings of emotional pressure and inadequacy that may leave long-standing wounds upon the emotional life. Similarly – and part of the same ground-rule – parents must not attempt to use the child against each other. This can happen at times even where the parental relationship is a strong one. No rivalry for the child's affections should ever be allowed to emerge, and no attempt be made by one partner to enlist the child as an ally against the other.

At yet another level, there is need for agreement on the child's spiritual education. Parents are the child's first teachers in all areas of life, and in no area is this more true than the spiritual. As the quote from Wordsworth emphasized at the beginning of the chapter, spirituality is something with which we are born, and not something that is grafted on to us as a result of what we are told. Thus children are conscious of themselves as spiritual beings from the first dawnings of self-awareness. What is meant by this early spiritual consciousness will be discussed in more detail later, but essentially it means that young children do not experience themselves as limited to their material bodies, or as bounded by the physical objects around them. The child inhabits a world of infinite possibilities, and the restrictions laid upon this world are placed there not by the developing mind, but by the words and actions of the adults who people that world.

Spirituality implies a way of being and not just a way of talking, a way of knowing and thinking and not just a way of behaving. It is difficult for two people to share a close and loving relationship for any length of time if one of them feels intensely this spirituality while the other takes a firmly materialistic path. And even within spirituality itself there can be important differences of emphasis and interpretation – as when, for example, two partners express different faiths. For the sake of the child, common ground and common understanding must be established before the birth. This does not mean that both partners must now pretend to be something they are not. What it means is that the partners must agree not to invalidate each other's beliefs in the eyes of the child, with all the damage this would do to the relationship itself, and all the confusions it would set up in the child's mind. What it also means is that where the partners differ markedly from each other in their spiritual outlook, and where one is not prepared to step back and leave the child's formal spiritual education to the other, there should be agreement that the child is reared in an openness that allows for eventual choice. This openness should always be there, even when the spiritual views of the partners are in complete accord, but it takes on added importance when each partner is travelling a different path.

Choice is part of the child's spiritual birthright, and although this birthright cannot be claimed during the very early years of life, the conditions for its eventual exercise must be put in place during these years. The various ways in which this can be done will be made clearer in the chapters to come.

THE CHILD AND OTHER CHILDREN

Up to now I have been talking only of parents during the months before the birth of a new baby. But often there are already older children or an older child in the family, and they must also be fully prepared for the coming event. Older brothers and sisters commonly have mixed feelings once a new addition arrives, even though they may be too young to put these feelings into words, or even to be fully in touch with them. Such feelings are a compound of excitement and pride on the one hand, and of doubt and insecurity on the other. For the very young, the new baby is like a toy, to be played with and enjoyed for a time, and then returned to the cupboard when one grows tired of it. The world as they have hitherto known and understood it does not contain a small sibling permanently on hand and demanding and obtaining parental attention, often at their own expense. Older children need time to come to terms with the major change that this introduces into their lives.

The problem is that through its need for love and attention, the new baby poses a threat to older brothers and sisters. It takes away some of the things – in particular undivided parental time and attention – which up to now have seemed rightly to belong to them. The very helplessness of the baby can also be a threat. Having learned to cope with many of the early skills of self-care, older children can be indignant at the baby's inability to fend for itself. The many tasks that they themselves are expected to do, seem not to be demanded of the baby. They are expected to tidy up after play, while it is allowed to mess with impunity. They are expected to follow instructions, while it is allowed to turn an apparently deaf ear to them. They are expected to be independent, while it is allowed to be so obviously dependent. Small wonder that older children feel there is one law for them and quite another – much more lenient one – for the baby.

The feelings of the older child are only natural, and deserve to be respected and accepted. Handled gently, they soon pass. Small children are adaptable people, and very soon they enlarge their sense of the world to include their new brother or sister. But if their feelings of rejection towards the baby are misinterpreted by parents and dealt with angrily and punitively, there is a real risk that these feelings will develop into deep-seated hostilities that will persist and sour the relationship between the two children for years to come. Some rivalry between siblings is inevitable and in many ways healthy, but there is a difference between rivalry based upon a genuine desire for competition and self-assertion, and rivalry based upon feelings of threat and injustice.

In the months and weeks before the arrival of the new baby, older children therefore need to be prepared for what lies ahead. This is best done by explaining the actualities of what mother and father will need to do in order to care for the new baby, and what their own role in this caring will be. Small children have practical minds. They are not ready for lengthy abstract discussions on the need to love each other, important as these may later become. Of far more use to them is a clear idea of what the daily routine is going to be like once the new baby has arrived, and of the extent to which both parents will need to rely upon them for help. Actual rehearsals are of enormous value, with mother or father bathing or changing or feeding a doll, and the older child given an interesting and responsible supporting role, and told how each parent will not be able to manage the new baby without his or her help. Young children like to feel significant and important (a feeling by no means confined to young children!), and it is crucial that their sense of significance should be enhanced rather than diminished with the coming of the new baby.

Thus older children are drawn fully into the experience of the new baby. They are included in discussions, their opinions are sought and their help enlisted at every possible opportunity. They have their say in how the new baby's room is to be arranged, and take part in the pleasant ritual of blessing the room. They are the first to announce to visitors that a new baby is on the way, and are asked their views on what clothes and toys to make or buy for it. If they are old enough, they prepare gifts of their own. They are introduced to the baby of neighbours or friends, and where possible this real baby is used in place of a doll during the rehearsals mentioned earlier.

In spite of this careful preparation, there will inevitably be *some* displays of jealousy once the new baby actually arrives. The response to these must be gentle and persuasive rather than angry and accusing. Where parents are regarded by older children as taking sides with the baby, the jealousy rapidly becomes worse, and if subdued by punishment will take the form of covert acts of spite against the baby, which are likely to be interpreted by adults as evidence of a wicked streak. In fact they are nothing of the kind.

The older child has to relieve his or her strong feelings in some way, and if doing so openly only attracts retribution, then attempts to do so in secret are bound to develop.

As far as possible, older children should be given as much parental attention as before, and must never be banished from the presence of parent and baby if they want to be included. Denied attention, an older child will quickly discover – through trial and error – that naughtiness is a sure way of winning it back. Parents are often puzzled by the fact that a child may prefer angry attention to being ignored, but there is no mystery about this. No matter how guilty the child may feel as a result, gaining angry attention is at least a way of feeling significant. To be ignored or sent away to mope on one's own when one wants company is to be relegated to a position of total unimportance in the eyes of others and of oneself.

Wise parenting is very much concerned with helping children know and understand all aspects of themselves, and with empowering them to exercise self-management through this understanding rather than through guilt and through repression of their natural feelings. Thus when experiencing jealousy the child should be helped to recognize what is happening in his or her emotional life, and this help can be given even at a very young age. The rule is that if children are old enough to express an emotion like jealousy, then they are old enough to begin the process of understanding where the emotion is coming from and how best it can be dealt with. The child can therefore be reassured that 'I know you feel a little bit jealous of the baby because he is taking up some of the time of all of us, but remember that mummy and daddy love you as much as ever, and I'm looking forward to coming and playing with you in a few minutes as much as you are'. Older children can also be told that they were once just as helpless as the baby, and needed just as much attention, and that if he or she had a choice, the baby would love to be as big and strong as the older child. The latter can also be reminded that soon the baby will be old enough to come and join in their games, and that this will mean more fun for everyone.

If the older child – as sometimes happens – attempts to hit the baby when it is being held by an adult, the baby must be protected, but to return violence for violence only leaves the older child feeling more rejected than ever, and teaches him or her the unfortunate lesson that violence is actually acceptable provided you are an adult and the other person is a child. Instead, while protecting the baby, the older child should be told that the baby isn't capable of self-defence, and that it's extra important we don't try and hurt him or her. This message is learned and accepted if it is given with gentleness and understanding. Gentleness towards the older child is the best way of teaching the lesson of gentleness towards the baby. And provided the older child is shown by actions as well as by words that parental love is as strong as ever, and that parental attention is readily available, the phase of jealousy will be short lived.

In addition to jealousy, an older child may at times revert to babyish behaviour, even to wetting the bed or becoming messy with food. However annoying this is for parents, it again is natural enough. The baby gets attention through wetting and messing, so it seems reasonable to the older child that the same will apply to him or her. To punish the older child on these occasions is simply to emphasize once again that there is one law for the baby and quite another for him or her. The correct response is a reminder that everyone thought the older child was so much more grown-up than the baby, and had long ago got beyond baby habits. This should be reinforced by seizing every opportunity to praise the older child for being so capable, and by assurances of how pleased everyone will be when the baby is old enough to behave like big brother or sister.

THE BABY'S FIRST MONTHS

If the preparations have proceeded satisfactorily, the new baby should come into an environment that is graced by tranquillity and peace. From the first, babies are very sensitive to loud noises, to rough handling, and to bright lights, finding them frightening and disturbing. In the next chapter I shall look much more closely at the world as the baby sees it, but from the early days of life onwards babies are much more aware of their surroundings than experts used to think. They can focus visually on objects some 20 cm (8 inches) away, and although anything nearer or further away is blurred, this is all to the good since it prevents them from being overwhelmed by too many stimuli at any one time. And a depth of focus of 20 cm is ideal in itself, since it allows them to see what is in fact the most important visual stimulus of all during the early months, namely the human face.

For reasons that we don't yet fully understand, babies quickly show a clear preference in these early months for certain objects and shapes over others. For example, complex shapes are preferred to simple shapes, and moving objects to stationary objects. The lesson the baby is teaching us is that from the very early stages of life, visual stimulation appears to be of great importance for his or her development. Deprived of this stimulation, it may be that the quality of a child's response to shapes and colours may be significantly restricted, perhaps permanently. In certain areas of development (for example, in the acquisition of language and of certain physical skills) there are critical periods during which the necessary learning can most effectively take place. If the child is denied the necessary stimuli during these periods, then this learning may never be accomplished as effectively in later life. There is a strong possibility that critical periods may exist also for the development of visual and auditory skills, hence the need to ensure that the child is from the first exposed to an environment that is as visually and auditorially interesting as possible, that contains pictures and mobiles, soft music and the sound of soothing voices, laughter and fun, safe soft toys, and that carries the message that the world is a beautiful and happy place into which to be born.

The same is true for the emotional environment. During the early months and years of life, a child goes through the process of bonding emotionally to those who care for him or her. This bonding is greatly strengthened if the baby sees as much of these care-givers as possible, and is given plenty of loving physical contact. Touch is of enormous importance to the young child, and is indeed the earliest form of language. Through touch the child is reassured of parental love and protection. Through touch he or she is allowed to feel safe and secure. Through touch the lesson of trust is learned, and through touch the baby comes to know and recognize parents and their particular ways of relating physically to him or her. Touch at all times should be gentle but (where appropriate) firm, and the baby allowed to explore with his own hands the faces and the bodies that he sees and against which he is held.

Babies are highly sensitive to the emotions of others. Rough handling and loud and angry voices upset them deeply. Almost from the moment of birth onwards the young child is an explorer, alert to what is happening in the world around and responding to it with deep levels of feeling. It is the quality of this feeling that tells a baby whether the world is a pleasant or unpleasant place, a happy or unhappy one. Spirituality implies love and tenderness. If the baby is to be introduced early to the spirituality of others, then long before he or she can understand words a peaceful, gentle and caring environment will begin to carry the message of this love. Such a message will arouse contented feelings in the young child, with the result not only that he or she will find life a welcoming experience but also that they will be much readier to reach out to the world instead of regarding it with fear and suspicion.

In Ecclesiastes we are told, 'Cast thy bread upon the waters, and thou shalt find it after many days.' In other words, whatever we give will in the fullness of time be returned to us, and in the spiritual life returned with abundance. In nothing is this truer than in the raising of a child. Every act of unselfish love, every act of patience, every gift of time will be repayed by a child tenfold in the years to come. How often have parents asked my advice about problems with older children, and then revealed after questioning the mistakes they made in the early years, and for which they are now paying a heavy price. My sympathy goes out to them. Well-meaning and concerned, they did what they thought was right, and the sad thing is that they were ignorant of the mistakes they were making. And how often have I heard them say that these mistakes were caused by their fear of 'spoiling' the child. The pity is that 'spoiling' is usually taken to mean over-indulgence, whereas far more real spoiling is done by imposing upon children the wrong kind of discipline, and by denying them the right to be themselves.

I began the chapter with a quotation from Wordsworth, the poet par excellence of childhood and of the wisdom of childhood, and I cannot do better than end with another. Telling of a conversation with the 5-year-old son of a friend he concludes with the lines:

> O dearest, dearest boy! my heart
> For better lore would seldom yearn,
> Could I but teach the hundredth part
> Of what from thee I learn.

CHAPTER 2

The Child's World

THE WORLD AS A CHILD SEES IT

I talked in the last chapter about the world as the new baby sees it, a world of colours, shapes and sounds that quickly begin to take on meaning. Much of this meaning comes through association. The baby is programmed by nature to respond with happy feelings to certain sensations, and these feelings become rapidly linked in his or her mind with the people who provide the sensations. Thus the pleasurable feelings aroused by feeding and by physical care and comfort, and by soothing sounds and the touch of gentle hands, become associated in the baby's mind with a mother's face, with the sound of her voice, with the warm smell of her body, and with the joy of her laughter. The baby thus learns early to discriminate mother from the rest of the environment and to respond to her with pleasure, and in a similar way to discriminate and respond to father and to other care-givers. As early as the third month of life, babies will in fact already be showing marked preferences for certain people over others. They will then go on to show preferences for the familiar things and experiences associated with these people, for the clothes and the colours they wear, for their activities around the house, for the chair in which they sit for feeding and nursing, for the fun at bathtime, and for the song at bedtime. In some ways, they are already beginning to see the world as adults see it.

But there is a major difference, and this difference carries great importance for parenting. It is a difference that persists until quite late in childhood, and only gives way in the face of repeated adult insistence that there is only one correct way in which to view reality.

The difference is that to the young child all things have consciousness, not just human beings. In a way, very young children see the world as their ancestors saw it long ago, or as certain unmechanized and shamanic communities still see it. To very young children the wind, the sun, the mountains, the soft toys on the bed, the household cat, the pet rabbit, are all alive in the same way in which they themselves are alive. Having consciousness themselves, they attribute it to everything else, and have no conception of what it might be like to be without human awareness.

The result is that young children live in an enchanted world where anything can happen – whether exciting or terrifying. To quote Wordsworth again, the young child grows:

> fostered alike by beauty and by fear.

Young children accept without question that the clock in the hall can speak if it wishes, that the wind has a voice, that the rain has taken a decision to fall, that the sandman comes at night to throw dust into tired eyes. They accept these things not by virtue of the stories we read to them and the tales we tell, but because these stories and tales confirm what they already know, and tell of the world as it really is.

Their awareness of living in the midst of enchantment is strengthened by the fact that everything is subject to a seemingly miraculous process of change and transformation. Day-time is transformed into night and night-time into day by the hands on the clock; joy is transformed into distress by a tumble in the garden; full plates of food are transformed into empty plates by the act of eating; a full bath is transformed into an empty bath by pulling out the plug; personal appearance is transformed by dressing and undressing; toys are transformed by breakage or by being pulled apart. And so on. Knowing nothing of the scientific 'laws' that underlie these changes, they seem to young children the result of spells cast by some unseen but dimly sensed power.

Small wonder then that a belief in magic comes easily to a child, since magic is very much the art of transformation ('. . . as if by magic'). To the child the spells cast by the wizard in the picture book are no different in kind from the spells cast by mother and by father when they switch on the light or start the car. In such a world, everything is possible, and nothing need remain what it seems.

In such a magical world there is no difficulty in believing that unseen presences lurk under beds and in dark corners, or that fairies dance at the bottom of the garden, or that Father Christmas brings a sack of toys down the chimney at Christmas time, or that

God lives somewhere up in the sky with a host of angels, or that a spirit watches over the life of each tree and each plant. Much of the wonder of childhood comes indeed from the very fact that the world seems such a strange and exciting place. A door in the wall passed each morning on the way to the shops would lead to unimaginable adventures if only one could open it. Toys wait only until everyone is sleeping before creeping out of the cupboard and playing their own games on the hearth rug. No one can doubt there are strange secrets hidden in the trees at the end of the road, and that children are only sent to bed so they will miss the moment when the best adventures of the day begin. Two lines of poetry by Walter de la Mare sum up a small part of the wonder that the world holds for young children, and the fierce longing they feel to be freed to take a full part in it all:

> 'No bed no bed' we shouted, and wheeled our eyes from home
> To where the green and laughing woods cried 'Come'.

Happy the parent who can re-enter this magical world when watching or playing with a young child. Not only does this re-entry help us better understand our children but it also allows us to discover again something about ourselves, something that has long been forgotten, like a deserted room at the top of the house that we come across again after many years, and where a dusty beam of sunlight picks out the books and the toys that once enchanted our lives. There between its comforting walls we recognize again the sweetness that comes from just being alive. And if we look long enough, we may be privileged to catch a glimpse of the small child we once were, lying full length on the floor absorbed in a favourite game.

THE CHILD'S IMAGINATION

This re-discovery of a child's-eye view of the world is important for parents because within it lie the seeds of our own and of our child's imagination, creative powers, and sense of the numinous – of the spiritual realities that go beyond faith and enter the realm of certainty. The parent's way of handling this world-view is a vital one, because done badly it can limit the child's horizons in a way that will persist throughout life. Why is this?

Imagination is that quality that allows us to picture or to listen to things that are not physically present. We take it very much for granted, and seldom ponder its true nature. In fact it is a very strange and wonderful gift, strange because evolutionary theories are hard pressed to account for it at all, and wonderful because it allows us to transcend the present moment and engage in memories, visions and plans, to write stories, to summon up solutions to problems, to paint pictures, to compose music, to dream up new inventions and to arrive at new scientific theories.

Imagination is very much the path into inner space. It is through imagination that we can go deeper into this space. It is through imagination that our sleep is brightened by dreams, and through imagination that we conceive of the future and of what we might become. All the great spiritual and mystical traditions have taught techniques to develop and put to good use the imagination, and one of the prime tasks alike of the young monk and of the sorcerer's apprentice was to develop the power of the imagination until it rendered the inner world as real – and as potent in terms of psychological and spiritual growth – as the outer one. For the ancient Egyptians and Greeks, imagination was a way of contacting those archetypal forces personified as the gods and goddesses and mythical heroes, while for the holy man or woman it is a way of meditating upon the image of the divine, and of receiving the divine qualities into oneself.

Curb or belittle the child's imagination, and we go a long way towards destroying his inner life and crippling his powers of creativity. With the best of intentions, we most of us as parents (and as teachers when school starts) want to share all we know with our children. We are anxious that they should acquire as quickly and as accurately as possible the facts and information that will help them cope with life and understand the world as the rest of us understand it. Unfortunately, in the process, we gradually squeeze out the child's view of the world and replace it with our own. We fall into the trap of regarding the child's view as necessarily inferior to that of adults, and as something that must be transcended with all possible speed.

This approach is part and parcel of the notion that there is something less authentic about childhood than about adult life, as if childhood is essentially an immature preparatory stage during which one prepares for the real business of living. Childhood is thus in a subtle way devalued. The childhood years are regarded not as a time that exists as much in its own right as do the years of adulthood, but as an introduction to real life that must be got through as quickly as possible. There is a sense in which young children are seen as less complete human beings than their elders and betters, as individuals who are not to be taken so seriously, as people who own less of themselves and who have less rights in the world than grown-ups.

Spiritual parenting starts from the belief that childhood is as valid a part of life, in and of itself, as adulthood. Spiritual parenting takes the view that learning between children and adults is a two-way process, with each becoming wiser and more human through knowing the other. Spiritual parenting tries to understand the full meaning of Christ's instructions to 'Suffer the little children to come unto me: for of such is the Kingdom of Heaven.'

This is not a way of saying that such parenting is about letting children see the world as they please, without teaching them the skills to live in and make use of our science-oriented culture. But it is a way of saying that this teaching should not deny the reality of the child's imaginative vision, and indeed should encourage him or her to develop and explore it as a vital resource now and for the future. Science has provided us with a deep understanding of the workings of some parts of the material world, but there are many things that science cannot do. There are vast areas of life into which it has not probed and for which it does not possess (and may never possess) the tools to probe. And the most important of these areas is the inner world of the mind. The result of this is that, rather like childhood as opposed to adulthood, the inner world has come to be regarded as of less importance than outer reality. Unless scientists can explore the mind in the way that they can explore material phenomena, they all too often choose to ignore its mysteries, and speak of it only as a by-product of the material, electrochemical activity of the brain.

And yet the mind is the country in which we each live our lives. We never move outside its borders. The mind is the country where we experience our joy and our suffering, where we think our thoughts and dream our dreams. The mind, in a very real sense, is who we are. Thus spiritual parenting cherishes the imaginative processes that go on in that mind, and although it teaches young children the difference between these processes and the rational and analytical thinking necessary to deal with the outer world, it does not elevate the latter *at the expense of* the former. It sees both as having their different – but equally necessary and important – place in the business of being alive.

DEVELOPING THE CHILD'S ACTIVE IMAGINATION

Imagination is an inborn ability, and like all inborn abilities it can be developed or – as I warned in the last section – stifled. Development can be helped in a number of ways. The first of these is very simple, yet lies at the heart of what has already been said and of much that is to follow. It is to respect the child's imaginative life, to listen to him when he talks about it, and to welcome the insights into his inner world with which it provides us.

The second is to join the child in this imaginative life, and the best way to do this is through stories. There is no substitute in these early years for reading to a child. The story, the spoken word, conjures up pictures in a child's mind in a manner that nothing else can do. Television, for all its usefulness in other ways, does very little for children's imagination, since it presents them with both words and pictures. They need bring nothing to the experience except emotional reactions. The images on the screen capture and hold their attention, but lack the creative power of their inner imaginings. Something similar happens for us as adults if we imagine the characters in a novel for ourselves, and afterwards see a dramatized version in the cinema or on television. The film of the book almost always has a certain flatness about it. The characters are not true to our own creations, and we feel disappointed with them for bearing frail comparison with the men and women who graced the living theatre of our minds.

Reading to children thus feeds their imagination in a unique way. They become totally immersed in the story; the boundaries between the everyday world and the world of their imagination dissolve, and the latter becomes as real to them as the former. This means we have to be careful over what stories we choose to read. We have no right to present to children only tame and sanitized material, because the stories we read should extend their experience and broaden their horizons. But in the absence in their minds of boundaries between fantasy and reality it is all too easy for the creatures and events in a story to step out of the pages and into their bedrooms. The fear engendered by certain stories can stay with a sensitive child for years – even into adult life.

When choosing material, one useful guideline is to remember the books we ourselves enjoyed as young children. In many cases the best stories follow familiar patterns. For example, they start with a situation of some kind, which is then disrupted by the arrival of some bad influence from outside (a dragon, the financial ruin of the father, a wicked uncle, a stepmother). As a result, the hero (who represents the archetype of the adventurous side of both male and female) decides to leave home and set out in search of a magical object of some kind (a 'fortune', a ring, a sword), which will restore the original happy state of affairs. After many adventures the object is found, the hero returns home in triumph, banishes or destroys the evil influence, and rather than simply restoring the original state of affairs effects a joyful transformation in the lives of family, town, or even the whole kingdom.

Such a story-line carries deep symbolic meaning. The original situation is a metaphor for childhood itself, and the intrusive influence is the disruption and change brought about as the child grows older and loses his or her original innocent vision of the world. The magical object represents wisdom or the discovery of man or womanhood or of spiritual insight – or at the very least of a conviction that life carries a grand purpose that must be discovered if we are to live happy and fulfilled lives – and the return in triumph at the end of the story stands for the transformation that such a discovery brings. Instead of a return to childhood, there is now the richness and the promise of adult life.

SYMBOLS AND ARCHETYPES

The child is, of course, unaware consciously of this symbolic meaning. But symbolism, which at its deepest level is the language of the unconscious, does not require that he or she should be. The story fits the child's innate awareness of how life is and how it may become. At birth the mind already contains what we might call a blueprint of what can be called the structural pattern of human psychological life. Carl Jung, the great Swiss psychologist and psychotherapist, talked of this pattern as consisting of *archetypes*, instinctual tendencies that are inherited along with the rest of our genetic endowments and that programme us to respond to existence in certain ways. These archetypes emerge into consciousness in the form of personalized images that are then variously admired, identified with, worshipped – or rejected – by the individual human mind.

There is, for example, the archetype of the hero, which I touched on a moment ago, which represents the innate adventurous, idealistic side of ourselves, and which prompts us to admire heroic behaviour in others. Another example is the archetype of the wise old man (often ruthlessly suppressed in the modern Western world, with its youth culture), which motivates us towards a lifelong quest for wisdom, and which leads us to seek for and listen to great teachers; there is the archetype of the mother, which contains the maternal instinct and which draws us towards the idea of the warm, sustaining, fertile matriarch, and the archetype of the divine child, which makes us cherish the spontaneous, creative, playful side of ourselves, and to recognize the spiritual wisdom of young children (though this recognition is again often suppressed in Western culture).

Stories that contain these archetypal figures are therefore the ones that have a most immediate, instinctive appeal to young children. They resonate with something already present in the young mind. This is the reason for the perennial appeal of many fairy stories, and of the great myths and legends of the world. So in reading to children, the right place to start is with fairy stories and the well-known and much-loved nursery rhymes that we found spoke most deeply to us when we too were young. Parents sometimes point out that many fairy stories have a dark side, usually associated with the intrusive influence appearing at the start of the story. A mother dies and is replaced by a wicked stepmother, a giant or a dragon comes on the scene and demands a sacrifice of young men and women, an evil magician tricks a poor widow out of her savings. This is true, and I have already stressed that we must be careful not to frighten children too deeply with the tales we tell. But not only does the dark side of fairy stories symbolize the disruptive power of the outside world but it also represents things that already lie within the domestic lives of most children.

To understand this, we must understand the ambivalent relationship that a child has with his parents. Most parents are at one and the same time the providers of love, care and safety on the one hand, and of authority, coercion and even conflict on the other. For small children, it is very difficult to reconcile these two sides of their mothers and fathers. Equally, it is difficult for them to reconcile their own feelings of love for their parents' nurturing side, and their feelings of anger for the controlling and restricting side. In many ways, stories help them to do this. The wicked stepmother or the wicked witch represents the 'cruel' side of the mother, while the good fairy represents the loving side. Similarly the wicked uncle or magician represents the 'cruel' side of the father, while the knight in armour represents the loving side. These symbols allow children not only to express and understand more their own darker emotions but also allow them to accept these emotions as a natural and even necessary side of life. They recognize it is all right to be angry with the wicked witch or the evil magician, all right to be afraid of them, all right to want to see them defeated by the young hero, who starts out with every disadvantage but who ends up victorious.

COMING TO TERMS WITH THE EMOTIONAL LIFE

As I shall stress again later, one of the essential features of all good parenting is to allow children to come to proper terms with their emotional life. There is a natural tendency on the part of adults to accept children's 'good' emotions (affection, pleasure, sympathy and so on) and to reject their 'bad' (fear, anger, jealousy and the like). Yet all emotions are there for a purpose, and none of them is necessarily either good or bad in itself. Goodness and badness are to do with how the emotion is used. Without fear and anger – which prompt us to run away or to stand and fight when we are threatened – the human race would not have survived down the centuries. Even jealousy is a natural response to losing something that we hold to be important, and used properly can help prompt us to protect those we love and the things we hold sacred.

If children are to come fully to know and understand themselves, they must be allowed to face the entire range of their emotional lives, and be helped to develop and use emotional energy in productive and socially acceptable ways. Children who are forced to repress certain emotions for fear of guilt or of parental anger or the withdrawal of parental love, live always partly in fear of their own inner selves. The repressed emotions come to represent an obscure and evil force lurking deep down, and ready to break out the moment they lose self-control. A major cause of neurosis and of psychological problems in childhood and in adult life is this sense of inner dread and insecurity, which eventually may have to be confronted and worked through with the help of appropriate counselling and psychotherapy.

The stories we read to children should therefore touch on all the emotions they feel in their own young lives. The heroes and heroines who fill the pages of these stories should allow the child to identify with them as individuals and with their adventures. Even the sadness that attends some stories – stories in which, for example, the hero fails in his quest, or loses his life or the life of someone he loves – is a necessary part of childhood. For all the joy that it contains, childhood is also tinged from the start with loss. This is not just the loss of innocence to which I have already referred, but the loss of friends who move away, the loss of pets or even of people close to the child like grandparents. Once children have encountered the possibility of loss, they need to come to terms with the fear it engenders. Will their parents disappear or die, and leave them alone in the world? Will a brother or a sister or a best friend do the same?

To hear about loss in stories helps the child to see that loss is a part of the lives of everyone. We all live in a world that is marked by insecurity. All the things we hold dear, including our own lives, are in reality on loan to us, and one day must be given back. Children should not be abruptly exposed to a knowledge of these profound but initially disturbing truths, but through story-books they are able to make gradual acquaintance with them, and are helped to see them not as enemies but as part of the constant process of change and renewal upon which human existence depends.

THE RHYTHM AND HARMONY OF LIFE

Given this help, children come to recognize that behind the insecurities of life there is a subtle harmony and rhythm in the sense of things combining together to create the world as we know it, an enriching pattern that properly understood produces an equal response in the human spirit. For young children there is great value in appreciating this early sense of harmony and rhythm. It enables them see life as fundamentally beautiful and in certain ways predictable, with all the reassurance and personal empowerment that predictability can bring. Young children are building up as it were a mental map of the world, a map that allows them to find their way through the mysteries of life, to relate to the things around them, to make everything work, to avoid pain and experience happiness, to perform well. An unpredictable world would mean that the map has constantly to be re-drawn, and would put doubts and confusions in young minds.

Nature herself is built upon the principles of harmony and rhythm. All her creations blend harmoniously into each other. Trees, mountains, rivers, clouds, the sunlight on water meadows – nature herself never fails the test of perfection. The rhythm of her seasons, of day and night, of sowing and harvesting, of youth and age, of in-breath and out-breath, make the world familiar, and allow us to know what the future holds, even though the uncertainty of our own lives means that we cannot predict the precise part we ourselves will play in it.

Since they are so much a part of nature, harmony and rhythm are also part of ourselves. Once we recognize their presence, our lives take on an inner security that allows us to meet the challenges that life has to offer. Children are much nearer to nature than we are. Without our portmanteau of concepts about the natural world, children can experience it directly and openly for what it is. To the child colours are colours, and not theories about how each surface absorbs and reflects the spectrum of visible light. To a child water is water, and not two parts hydrogen and one part oxygen. To a child the sun circles the earth, and the moon and the stars come out at night. However naive we may feel this vision of nature to be, it is an accurate representation of how we actually *experience* her. By responding directly to nature rather than to facts and formulae and abstract concepts about her, the child responds more intimately to her, and in a real sense is wiser in her ways that we are.

Blessed with this closeness to nature, a child responds immediately to her harmony and her rhythm. The wise parent knows and fosters this closeness, looking and listening to nature together with the child. This means taking the child as often as possible to green places, sitting in the shade of trees and listening to bird song and the sound of wind in the branches. It means helping children to use their eyes, to collect leaves and stones and other gifts of nature, to look at the red sunset low in the evening sky and the moon riding high at night. It means enjoying together the scents of nature, the breeze off the sea, the red rose and the honeysuckle in the garden, the green lawn newly cut and the sweet smoke of incense.

A child's natural gift for appreciating nature is thus fed by the wise guidance of parents, and in giving this guidance parents are in turn fed by the open joy of their child. Watch a small child absorbed in nature, and see in his or her total concentration the captivating wonder of natural things. See a child follow the progress of a caterpillar along a twig, dig in the sand of the seashore and gaze at the water flowing into the hollow, pick a flower and look long at its delicate beauty. Watch a child actively engage with nature, and see the joy a child takes in physical movement and in the sensation of touch; running through long grass, splashing in the shallows at the margins of the sea, holding and fondling a domestic pet, indulging in mock physical combat with young friends. Watch these things, and recognize the power of nature to lift the spirits, to whisper her secrets, to reassure us that we are not alone in the world but an integral part of a single living system that stretches from the smallest insect to the remotest star. To see nature once more through the eyes of a child is to rediscover something we once knew but have long forgotten, that because of our oneness with all creation there are no limits to our true state of being.

CHAPTER 3

Learning and Growing: I

THE TASKS OF CHILDHOOD

A child brings a great deal into the world, and takes, in the form of learning, a great deal from it. We can think of this learning as a number of key tasks, each of which should be accomplished successfully before the child goes on to the next. These tasks are like the various levels in a beautiful building, with each level crowning those below and providing a foundation for those above. Should any of these levels be shaky, those above are bound to suffer, and the whole building rendered unstable and prone to problems. The tasks themselves are less to do with the acquisition of factual knowledge (although factual knowledge is vital in its place, and I have something to say about it in Chapter 5), than with the creation of selfhood, that is with the whole way in which life is experienced, including a sense of personal worth and of happiness, and the ability to enter into intimate, unselfish, and honest relationships with others. Selfhood encompasses personality as well as a sense of personal identity, and it has much to do with whether life is experienced as fulfilling and meaningful, or as ultimately fragmented, unsatisfactory, and hollow.

Erik Erikson, famous for his work on the psychology of child development, proposed that these tasks – each of which is particular to a separate stage of growth through childhood and into adolescence – can be described as follows (the ages given for each stage are approximate):

trust (early infancy, 0–2 years)
autonomy (late infancy, 2–4 years)
initiative (early childhood, 4–6 years)
competence (middle childhood, 6–12 years)
identity (adolescence, 12–18 years)

Let's take each of these tasks in turn and see what it means for the child and his or her parents.

TRUST

By developing trust in their parents and other care-givers, children learn they can safely rely on the ability of the adults in their lives to provide for their physical and emotional needs. Young children who are denied the chance to develop trust cannot help but view the world with suspicion and unease. Dependent upon temperament (pages 55–7), they may in consequence become anxious and withdrawn, or hostile and aggressive. Either way, the world will become to them a disturbing and threatening place.

A generous minimum of care, of love and of understanding on the part of parents and care-givers is necessary for the development of trust. Even as adults we prize the presence of family and friends on whom we can depend completely. The development of trust reassures children that they are protected and safe, and provides them with a sound base from which to go out and explore the world. Provided children are sure they have this base to which they can return at need, they are much less likely to act aggressively or defensively towards life, or to stay huddled in their own small corner. Children are naturally curious, naturally eager as soon as they can crawl to set off on journeys of discovery. The only encouragement they need is the certainty that they are loved and cherished, and will be protected whenever they come up against real harm.

Trust also allows children to begin the process of creating mature relationships with others. In the first months, their relationships are dominated by a need for the basic necessities of life such as nourishment and comfort. They have no concept of others as separate individuals with lives and needs of their own. But during the second year of life children begin to see their parents and care-givers as real people. Provided trust is developing, this means that their relationships with parents during the second year become immeasurably enriched, and provide them with a favourable beginning for the whole socialization process.

If children learn that their parents are to be trusted, they are encouraged to reach out also to the other people in their lives. Some children are by nature more sociable than others, but to be human is to be born with a spontaneous and joyful urge towards the rest of the human race. We are a gregarious species. But children who are isolated and neglected in the early years of life progressively – and tragically – lose much of this urge. Even the excessive clinging behaviour shown by some children is a sign that the socialization process is not proceeding as it should. They hold fast to their parents or those around them because they cannot trust to place themselves in the hands of others, and – more sadly still – because they cannot trust even the people they know not to abandon them the moment they are allowed to move out of sight.

AUTONOMY

Autonomy is the sense that we have a right to be ourselves. It emerges during the third year of life, when children first become conscious of themselves as individuals with lives of their own, and with the ability to *choose* what they want to do, instead of being governed only by basic physical needs or by the actions of other people. From now on, they recognize in themselves the existence of free-will, and as with any exciting discovery, they want to put it to immediate and effective use. Thus in the third year children often go through a highly negative phase in which they become obstinate and disagreeable apparently for the sake of it. Every suggestion made by long-suffering parents is greeted with scorn, their minds change on the whim of the moment, and the impression is conveyed to all and sundry that they are put into the world primarily to test the sanity of the rest of the human race.

Wise parents see this negative phase not as a sign that the devil is in the child (as did some earlier generations), but as a natural indication of the development of the self. In fact – for all the problems this phase can cause – it is a welcome sign, since children who do not pass through it often appear later in childhood as lacking in spirit and as easily led. The determination and courage (yes courage – after all, it is not easy to stand up for yourself when you are not yet 3 years old!) shown by the child at this time are, if we think about it, among the very qualities most admired in adult life. This emphasizes a very important truth about childhood, namely that it is precisely those things that make children appear difficult (we can add to determination and courage such attributes as creativity, individuality and leadership) that will one day make them effective and admired members of society. Parents who recognize this rely primarily upon guidance, persuasion and co-operation in order to deal with the negative three-year-old rather than upon force, authoritarianism, and those constant battles of wills which leave everyone guilty and exhausted.

During the third year of life, children also begin to distinguish and recognize their own emotions. Previously they were aware only of bodily sensations, some pleasant and some unpleasant – comfort, hunger, satiation, thirst, tiredness – but now they become conscious of the emotional responses that arise in response to these sensations and, increasingly, in response to more complex and more subtle stimuli. Excitement on opening Christmas presents, for example, frustration caused by other children, anger on being prevented from doing as they wish, disappointment when denied a special treat, joy on playing games or splashing about in water, fear on being lost in a crowd, interest on listening to a story, and so on. This recognition further emphasizes the sense of selfhood.

INITIATIVE

Each one of us, no matter how apparently uneventful our years, leaves a permanent mark upon the world. Even the simple act of kicking a stone across the road permanently changes the way in which the world is arranged. In a sense, each act of our lives is thus an act of initiative, an *initium*, an origination, a placing of something new upon the turning face of history. But, of course, there are varying kinds of initiative, and the most important are usually those that spring from a conscious intention to alter things for the better. And like all initiatives, these have their origins in the growth of self-will in childhood. For once having discovered that they have a mind of their own, children are now in a position to decide where and how to put it to use.

The presence of initiative is, like the emergence of self-will, something to be welcomed in our children. Certainly children have to learn how to select initiatives that are appropriate, and how to reject those that are not, but it is vital they be allowed to recognize that initiative *per se* is an invaluable, essential, part of life. For this recognition to take place, the early acts of initiative shown by the child from the third year onwards must be acknowledged, encouraged, and wherever possible put to good use. The initiative, for example, that prompts a child to rush willingly (if somewhat chaotically) to help when elders are engaged on some task or other. The initiative children show when deciding what games to play, what clothes to wear, what walks to take, what stories to hear, what greeting to offer to visitors, what pictures to draw. Curb this initiative by constantly trying to direct the child in the way of our own likes and dislikes, and we will not only be frustrating him or her but also curbing the initiative on which the quality of their lives and of the lives of those close to them will in the future to large measure depend.

COMPETENCE

Competence is the direction in which initiative should properly go. Having learned that they have self-will and the power to make choices, children now need to learn how to operate this power to good effect. They have in other words to learn how to do things well. Middle childhood is a time when school becomes an increasingly important influence upon a child's development. He or she is now exposed not just to the expectations of adults but to those of children of their own age. It is sometimes hard in adult life to remember how daunting it was to find ourselves as children performing badly in comparison with others. A young child's sense of self is still very new and fragile. There is a knowledge of being a distinct person, but little knowledge of what *kind* of person. A successful or unsuccessful one, popular or unpopular? effective or ineffective? Placed in an environment where everyone else seems more competent and assured, a child inevitably comes to rate him- or herself negatively, and suffer painful feelings of inadequacy, humiliation and despair.

Things are made worse if teachers and parents also indicate they find a child inadequate. Since as yet children have no clear picture of who they are, they take over this picture from others. If they are told – by action if not by word – that they are slow or silly or stupid, then they come to believe it, no matter how able they may actually be. And this belief, once established, will prove remarkably resistant to change in the future, no matter how much success life brings. Many a highly respected adult seeks psychological help in the middle years because of nagging feelings of inadequacy that date back to parents who were never satisfied, no matter how well he or she performed. It would be wrong to say that our picture of ourselves is finalized during childhood, but the outlines and much of the detail are painted in during these years, and the job of altering the picture into a more accurate likeness later on can be a long and arduous one.

Young children therefore need at all times to be helped to gain competence by emphasizing to them the things they can do rather than the things they can't. They learn best through success rather than through failure. Each task they are asked to do should be within their ability and not beyond it. Standards are raised and augmented by starting from where the child is now, and going on from there. Giving children something they are unable, with their present level of ability and powers of concentration, to do and then blaming them for not being able to do it (as happens in many homes and schools) is a sure recipe for damaging their self-esteem and ultimately for making life more difficult for themselves and for those with whom they live. Dependent upon temperament, a child who experiences mostly failure will either withdraw increasingly in sadness and self-rejection, or become defensive and rebellious towards everything to do with effort and attainment. In both cases, the psychological wound goes deep, no matter how aggressively it is covered up. It is unfortunately all too true that if someone shows me a problem child, I will show them a child who has been denied the proper opportunity to recognize his or her own worth.

At a practical level, the wise parent, when criticizing children, refrains from labelling them, and refers instead to their actions. There is a world of difference between being told *you are a silly child* and being told *that was a silly thing to do*. The former remark says something about you as a person, the second says something about what you have done. The former leaves you feeling that silliness is part of your nature, the latter implies you have chosen unwisely and next time can be better. Labelling a child contributes to a negative self-image. Describing a child's actions, while indicating where things have gone wrong, leaves the self-image unimpaired.

COMPETENCE AND THE SENSE OF RIGHT AND WRONG

Competence, and the self-esteem that depends so closely upon it, is important not only in relation to the knowledge and skills needed to cope with life but also to the development of a sense of right and wrong. A sense of right and wrong – a sense of morality – depends crucially upon the power of choice. Choice, as we saw earlier, is something that emerges only when children become conscious of themselves and of the presence of free-will. Thus from around age three onwards the foundations of moral behaviour are being laid. But initially this behaviour comes not from a true appreciation of right and wrong, but from an awareness of what adults expect. However, from around age 6 or 7 years, a true moral sense begins to develop, and the child becomes able to start questioning why certain things are right and others are not.

As in all areas of competence, the first priority in moral development is that we should expect of children only those things of which they are capable. This means requiring from them only those moral behaviours appropriate for a child of their age. Young children have very little impulse control and very short memories. They can't be expected always to resist temptations when they are unsupervised, or to remember exactly what they are and are not allowed to do. If as adults we find ourselves constantly reprimanding them for being in the wrong, we can be sure that too much is being asked of them. Good parenting requires that the child is early given the realization that moral behaviour is not an impossible or even an over-demanding task, but is simply a fair and sensible way of managing behaviour. Such realization can only be attained if, at each stage of development, the child is allowed to function in a moral environment appropriate to his or her powers of thinking, remembering and acting.

It is useful to stress that the point made earlier concerning the unsuitability of negative labels applies here too. Young children cannot develop a mature moral sense if they are constantly told that the fault lies in themselves rather than in their choice of actions. Similarly, they cannot develop a mature moral sense unless they are consistently helped to understand *why* certain actions are preferable to certain others. This may seem to demand a lot from parents, but like all aspects of good parenting it soon brings its own rewards, in that the child is able much earlier to begin to take responsibility for his or her own actions. It also helps parents in that it prompts them to look more closely at what they expect from their child. Once we start to do this, we are apt to discover that many of these things have far more to do with our own convenience than with moral issues of right and wrong. We have every justification for studying our own convenience from time to time, but problems arise if we confuse this convenience with morality. Right and wrong then risk being reduced to what suits or does not suit ourselves, and the child is given little real insight into their true meaning.

By looking more closely at the behaviour we expect of a child, we may also discover that even the things we consider true moral imperatives begin to look a little suspect. Many of our moral ideas are carried over from our own childhood, and some of them may be overdue for revision. Moral ideas often for good reason change from generation to generation with changing social conditions, while others need re-interpretation. Still others are built on the prejudices, however sincerely held, of our elders. My grandfather, an intelligent and thoughtful man, would refuse to take a Sunday newspaper because he maintained it involved journalists and printers labouring on the Sabbath, and in vain did we plead with him that in fact they worked on Sunday to produce *Monday's* edition (which after his day of fasting from newsprint he would always read with particular attention).

IDENTITY

The last of the tasks of the pre-adult years is the development of a mature sense of who we are. This is the culmination of the process that began with the first dawnings of the sense of self in the third year of life. Perhaps 'culmination' isn't the right word, for reasons touched on in the next paragraph, but the process reaches a particular intensity in adolescence, and many of the apparent problems and difficulties faced at that time are related directly to it. In adolescence, the individual stands poised between childhood and adulthood. Having learned, with varying degrees of success, how to cope with being a child, he or she now has to learn how to cope with being an adult. If we are to be of help to our children at this time we need to recognize the self-doubt and vulnerability that this learning can entail, and accept that adolescence is in fact second only to early childhood in its importance as a formative period of life. For the way in which the adolescent resolves the search for identity can leave a profound impression on the personality both now and in the future.

The search for identity is in fact one of the central psychological and spiritual tasks of life, a task which is rendered more difficult by the fact that although we know the importance of the search, we are rarely sure where we should actually be looking. Identity seems at times to exist at many different levels, and to be subject to constant change – to such an extent in fact that we may be left wondering whether it exists at all in any permanent sense. Even as mature adults we may be aware of one identity at work and a different one at home, one identity in the gloom of mid-winter and another on holiday in summer. And looking back over the years we may be aware of the extent to which, with changing relationships, commitments and responsibilities, our identity has undergone major changes as time goes by.

Awareness of the adolescent's search for identity can be a powerful stimulus for parents to look once more at how their own lives are progressing. In childhood and adolescence we ask constant questions about ourselves and about the world, but in later years we often tend to fall back on habit. We think we know ourselves because we have been around for a long time, and have become accustomed to our usual ways of feeling and thinking. In many cases it is only as the years go by and we realize that our time on earth is limited that we begin once again to ponder existential questions about the meaning of life and the realities of our own nature. Carl Jung, one of the founders of modern psychotherapy, commented that the psychological problems that people in their middle and later years presented to him invariably turned out to be religious ones at bottom, by which he meant that they had to do with an inner search for some conviction that ultimately life has a meaning to it beyond the purely physical.

WHAT IS IDENTITY?

Once we begin to look closely at the various levels at which identity operates, we become aware of just how different are the self-images concerned, and perhaps the sets of beliefs and values that go with them. At work we may think of ourselves as business-like and assured, a good leader and confident of our ability to handle the tasks in front of us. We may believe our relationships with colleagues should be formal and rather distant, and that the principles guiding our decisions should be dictated by professional rather than personal considerations. We may measure our worth by the extent to which we can get the best out of people, provide them with clear leadership, and believe that the best way to help them to succeed is by being successful ourselves.

At home on the other hand, our self-image will be governed by personal rather than professional considerations. Whereas emotions may play little part in determining our behaviour at work, at home they may often take precedence over everything else, including our rational judgements. In contrast to the working environment, we may recognize that our relationships at home depend upon the giving and receiving of love, and upon the involvement we show towards our family.

Another aspect of our self-image will have to do with such things as our membership of clubs or of a church or of societies, and with our leisure or part-time interests in general. Another part may have to do with our membership of a political party, and yet another with our relationships with friends, with next-door neighbours, and with the members of our extended family. In each of these contexts we will tend to think of ourselves in different ways. We may see ourselves as confident and successful in one of them, as diffident and unsuccessful in another, as straightforward and principled in one, as opportunist and a little devious in another, as patient in one and as impatient in another, and so on. Small wonder that people who know us in different settings may see different sides of us. Only when we come to examine ourselves in this way do we recognize how much of our public identity is socially determined, and how inconsistent can be the face we turn towards the world.

PRIVATE IDENTITY

At a deeper level than what we can call our public identity we have our private identity. This is the person we feel ourselves to be when we are metaphorically in the privacy of our own room. Naturally, private identity is strongly influenced by public identity. We carry over into our private moments the memories and emotions sparked off by our social encounters. But our private identity is more than this. It contains also our personal history, our secret hopes and fears, and the joys and embarrassments and misgivings that have elated or disturbed us across the years and which remain uniquely ours. It contains also the experiences that may be too precious or too painful to share with anyone else, however close they may be. Above all, it contains our intimate, unspoken sense of our own worth.

As with the public identity, the private identity can vary in both the short- and the long-term. Sometimes we may feel happy with ourselves, satisfied with what we are doing in life and the person we feel ourselves to be. At other times we may experience irritation and self-doubt. We can go from pride to disappointment, from elation to depression, from pessimism to optimism. Our private identity is essentially how we experience ourselves at any one point in time, and how we formulate the values and descriptions we place upon this experience. Even to the most stable of us, these values and descriptions, like those associated with our public identity, rarely remains consistent for very long.

Identity is therefore a fluctuating thing. Equally to the point, it is a fragile thing. A man or woman made suddenly redundant after many years in a particular job may overnight change fundamentally their view of themselves. The experience of being summarily rejected, even when the fault is transparently not their own, can reduce overnight their self-esteem, their sense of their value to others, and even their sense of significance as human beings. Similarly, the termination of a romantic relationship can be devastating for identity. At one moment we see ourselves as worthy of the love of the person we care for most in the world, and the next we see ourselves as of little consequence to them.

If our own identity is subject to such uncertainties, how much more is this true of the adolescent. At this time, acceptance by friends, by the peer group, by members of the opposite sex, becomes of enormous importance. Without such acceptance, adolescents see themselves quite literally as unlikeable and unlovable. And if others don't accept them at such a critical time, then it is hardly surprising that they find it impossible to accept themselves. Even for a popular adolescent, a momentary feeling of rejection by a best friend or by the group can lead to deep gloom and despondency, and a tendency to take out hurt feelings on the innocent members of one's own family. The situation is rendered even more difficult by the fact that at adolescence, puberty releases strange and powerful new emotions. Sexual arousal is the most obvious, but this is accompanied by likes and dislikes, attractions and revulsions, highs and lows that are unmatched for intensity at any other stage in life. As adults it is often difficult for us to remember the sheer compulsion of adolescent emotions, and even if memories still linger, we tend to pass them off as representing merely a phase – and an awkward one at that – in the confused business of 'growing up'.

But adolescence is as much a part of life in its own right as is childhood and adulthood. Indeed in adolescence, as in childhood, our sheer zest for life may have a strength unrivalled in the years to come. In adolescence we touch peaks of feeling that give life a magic that it may never recapture, no matter how rich the experiences that lie ahead. When talking to parents I cannot emphasize too strongly that each stage of life, each year of life, each hour and each minute, has a validity of its own. Life is not intended as an experience that builds to a climax in the middle years, thus forming an existential triangle with an uphill climb in childhood and adolescence and a downward slope in old age. Life consists only of each present moment, and the quality of experience that each moment brings. Childhood and adolescence can bring a richness of being, and sometimes a wisdom and a depth of insight, that are capable of matching and perhaps surpassing anything given to us in maturer years.

The wise parent never loses sight of this fact, and is aware that although the adolescent still needs parental support and guidance, this must be coupled at each point with a gradual letting go. To let go of our children is often one of the hardest things that life asks of us, but it is one of the most essential. From the moment of birth onwards children grow towards independence, and the final steps must be taken in adolescence and early adult life. In practical terms, letting go means allowing the relationship between parent and adolescent to move towards equality and away from parental authority. To move towards advice and debate and the exchange of opinions, and away from direction and stipulation. Throughout nature there comes a point where the young are ready to leave their childhood home, and however painful this can be for parents, we must accept it not only as the natural but as the proper order of things.

The desire of children to leave home does not, however, mean a rejection of their family and their earlier years. Parents sometimes feel their children are ungrateful in wanting to go to a distant university, or to a job in another town, instead of studying or working from home. After building a home for their children, and caring for them within it for so long, it seems that children want to throw everything away. I usually reassure parents that it is precisely because they have made such a good home for their children that the latter feel confident enough to spread their wings. It is akin to the confidence that comes to the very small child through the growth of trust (pages 32–3). A secure base is the very thing that emboldens the young to set off metaphorically to seek their fortune.

Of course there are occasions when an adolescent wants to leave home to escape unhappiness, or when he or she has romantic, unrealistic dreams that life is going to be more exciting in the big city. But if the proper foundations have been laid in earlier years, reasons of this kind are unusual. The adolescent simply wants to make his or her own way in the world. And the sensible parent realizes that although our children may always seem to us to be children, time has passed, the metamorphosis has taken place, and they have now emerged full-grown. (The subject of letting go is returned to again in Chapter 9.)

SPIRITUAL IDENTITY

In addition to public and private identities, there is a third, more elusive level, which we call the spiritual level. This is the level – more strongly realized in some people than in others – which has to do with the conviction that there is a part of us beyond or outside the ever-changing flux of our public and private worlds; that there is a consistency, an identifiable quality that is hard to express but which represents truly who we are. The conviction may come to us in dreams, or when we are listening to music or reading poetry, or enjoying the beauties of nature, or simply when we turn our attention inwards in meditation. In trying to find words for this feeling, people sometimes refer to it simply as a contemplative awareness, a still centre apart from – and capable of observing – our public and private worlds.

Buddhism has a doctrine known as *anatta*, a term that is difficult to translate but which is sometimes taken to mean that men and women have no permanent self. Westerners often suppose that Buddhism therefore teaches there is nothing to us beyond the moving, transient flow of our public and private experience, that life is merely a shifting panorama of thoughts and sensations that ends with the death of our physical bodies. If this were really what Buddhism is saying, it would never have taken the profound hold over the human mind that for over two thousand years it undoubtedly has. The doctrine of *anatta* in reality tells us not that we are simply a succession of physical and mental events, but that it is wrong to take this succession of events – our public and private identities – as representing our ultimate reality. These identities are indeed artificial, impermanent constructions, and enlightenment (or spiritual salvation if you prefer), lies in seeing the truth of this, and in transcending these constructions in order to discover what lies beyond.

Nothing can accurately be said about this beyond, since to try to express it in words is to subject it to the limitations of our finite language. However, since we have to use language, different traditions refer to it variously as nirvana, as paradise, as the kingdom of heaven, as the isles of the blessed. Some of these traditions teach that we find it through an act of grace that comes to us from outside, others that we find it from within ourselves. But if we listen to the teachings of the mystics, we learn that ultimately there is no difference between what comes from outside and what comes from within, that in truth reality is infinite and has no boundaries, and that in touching it we recognize and pass beyond the limits of the artificial self.

In adolescence, there is often a very vocal rejection of this third, spiritual identity. The adolescent will proclaim him- or herself as a hard-nosed materialist, scornful of the superstition of religion in any shape or form, and more inclined to put to rights the inequalities and iniquities of the real world than to be concerned with the shadowy uncertainties of the spiritual one. Such a volte face in a son or daughter who has previously been a dutiful member of the local church or temple or mosque can be very upsetting for parents. Yet what is happening is that in many cases adolescents, with their newly acquired ability for logical debate and for abstract thinking, have identified what they take to be inconsistencies and incredibilities in the religious teachings with which they have grown up. Very much involved in putting away childish things, adolescents often need a period of doubt during which to develop their own views and beliefs instead of clinging only to those received earlier from their elders.

In fact unless they go through this phase, it is doubtful if some adolescents will ever be able to develop a mature spirituality. The axiom 'doubt in order to be more certain' at no time carries greater truth than in adolescence. Only by an honest reappraisal of the beliefs fostered in childhood, and a rejection of those aspects of them that fail to stand up to scrutiny, can adolescents arrive in due course at a spirituality that they can claim as their own. As parents we need to accept this, and refrain from forcing our adolescent sons and daughters to retain beliefs they would prefer to discard. We need to place the emphasis upon debate, upon a readiness to respect the adolescent's point of view, and upon an avoidance of unnecessary recriminations or the arousal of a misplaced sense of guilt.

By contrast, other adolescents may go through an intensely religious phase, in which they enter into deep commitments to their beliefs. This again is natural enough. Adolescence is a period of extremes. On the threshold of the adult world, and fired with powerful inner enthusiasms, the adolescent is often driven to enter fully into any endeavour. Aware now of many of the shortcomings in the world, he or she sometimes feels in possession of the strength to bring about great changes. The future stretches ahead, ideals and ambitions are felt with particular intensity, and the sense of a special mission in life, a special goal to achieve, special mountains to climb, may be particularly strong.

Yet other adolescents go through a period of apathy, when nothing seems to capture their interest. This, in a different way, is also natural. The adolescent suddenly finds that the enthusiasms and delights of childhood have lost their appeal, and as yet there is nothing to take their place. Life seems empty and strange, and lectures from teachers and parents on what they 'should' be doing or feeling only tend to make things worse. Adolescents are not yet masters of their feelings. Their very moodiness is often more of a puzzle to them than it is to everyone else. Caught in an uneasy time-warp between childhood and man- and womanhood, they are doubtful and uncertain about life and about their place within it. Sometimes this doubt and uncertainty is accompanied by a seeming coldness and impatience towards parents, and a surliness of manner that may be in marked contrast to their previous behaviour.

Parents naturally worry about these and other phases through which their adolescent sons and daughters go. But most of these phases are temporary. With a little patience and understanding from adults, the adolescent soon comes to a new self-understanding and a more reasoned and balanced view of the world and of other people. Given greater independence and responsibility, and allowed to discuss and contract over such things as spending money, helping in the house, coming home in the evenings and other possible points of friction, the adolescent is enabled to forge new and positive relationships with parents and (equally importantly) with him- or herself.

CHAPTER 4

Learning and Growing: II

OTHER TASKS OF CHILDHOOD AND ADOLESCENCE

These five tasks of childhood and adolescence that we have been discussing must be seen against the background of three further tasks, which overarch and in part depend upon them, and run right through the formative years. These have to do respectively with learning self-control, learning to love (including how to handle sexuality), and learning to co-operate. Self-control is the readiness to take responsibility for one's own actions, and to have the strength to choose and direct them. Love and co-operation are to do with that extended sense of self that allows us to feel passionately and deeply for others, and to see their happiness and well-being as of equal importance to our own. Let's look first at self-control.

SELF-CONTROL

There are two reasons for learning self-control, one social and the other individual. The social reason is that self-control allows us to respect the needs of others and operate in the world unselfishly, and the individual reason is that self-control enables us to discipline ourselves to use the talents and abilities with which life has graced us. It is easy to see how both are linked to the sense of responsibility and to the sense of morality mentioned earlier. We have a responsibility and a moral duty towards others and towards our own potential, and neither of these can be properly discharged unless we learn to control and use ourselves and our time to proper effect. Self-control is very different from the rigid discipline that comes from over-strict and authoritarian parenting. As implied earlier, it comes through understanding and through choice. An understanding as to why certain behaviours are desirable rather than others, and an ability to choose these behaviours although at times they may represent the most difficult option.

Good parenting helps the child towards self-control not only by emphasizing an understanding of the needs of others and the growth of responsibility and of choice but also by paying the attention described above to the growth of identity. A developed sense of identity allows children to recognize their own strengths and weaknesses, and to acknowledge those areas of life where self-control proves difficult. Once acknowledged, these areas can be given the attention they need in ways described in Chapter 3. It is unfortunately true that usually our minds are not fully in contact with our emotions, with the result that we risk being overwhelmed at times by them, almost as if they arise unbidden from some unknown part of our own being. Self-control, in the proper meaning of the term, implies that we make this contact in order to bring the head and the heart into communication with each other. This is very different from fighting our emotions, or denying (to others and worse still to ourselves) that we are experiencing them. Such denial involves repression rather than mature self-control. It prevents us from being properly in charge of who we are, and using our emotions to serve us rather than to threaten and frighten us.

Some people suggest self-control risks making us cold and calculating, and lacking in human warmth and spontaneity. Nothing could be further from the truth. Emotions are an essential part of being human, and as mentioned earlier, it is important that we accept and respect their existence in our children. Self-control implies instead a proper balance between our thoughts and our feelings. It prevents us from acting always upon impulse, from following our own interests at the expense of those of others, from losing control over our behaviour and forfeiting the power of choice, which is one of the things that sets man apart from the rest of creation.

Children are born with the potential for self-control, but not with self-control itself. As mentioned earlier, they have little ability in the early years to control their impulses. Nor can they learn self-control through force. Rigid discipline simply breeds unthinking obedience, and relies upon the repression mentioned in the last paragraph – one of the most damaging of all psychological mechanisms. True self-control comes from a harmony within the self, an absence of the fragmentation and conflict that occurs when each part of our being attempts to pull in a different direction. It is an expression of a unified self, intent upon serving to the full the mysterious gift of human life.

LOVE

The most powerful and wonderful of emotions, it comes as a surprise to most people that the ability to love has in part to be learned. Children are born with a great potential for love, but like any potential, the degree to which it is developed depends very much upon the environment. In the first years of life (particularly the first two), a process called *bonding* takes place, during which as explained at the beginning of the last chapter the child's affections are increasingly centred upon the primary care-giver or care-givers (usually one or both of his parents). For full bonding to happen, however, the child needs a generous minimum of human contact, human attention, human love during these two early years. Without these gifts, children cease to reach out warmly and spontaneously towards the world, and withdraw emotionally, either viewing others with suspicion or fear, or demanding aggressively the attention that should be theirs by right. There are few more distressing sights than a small child who has been starved of love, and who sits lonely and neglected, often rocking sadly and rhythmically as the only source of comfort. Full bonding therefore demands that a child be frequently picked up and held close, frequently played with, talked to, sung to, laughed with, and generally allowed to feel surrounded by love, and a source of delight to everyone around.

Bonding is of course very closely associated with the growth in these first two years of trust. The child both bonds and trusts in response to consistent and loving parental care. And like trust, bonding provides the firm foundation upon which later personal and emotional development takes place. Successful bonding enables children to see other people as giving and caring, and as prompting deeply satisfying feelings within oneself. They are then free to go on and learn the more detailed aspects of love that have to do with gratitude, with unselfishness, forebearance, companionship, honesty, communication, and with understanding, acceptance, compassion and sharing – those aspects of love in short that reach beyond the immediate family circle and embrace progressively friends, acquaintances, strangers, and finally humanity in general.

By being loved in a mature and unselfish way, we experience the true meaning of love, and realize our own potential to give such love to others. However, if love is given to children conditionally and made dependent always upon parental approval, or if is inconsistent or demanding and selfish, or smothers and over-protects, their own capacity for love is in turn limited and distorted. They learn that love is something that must be given as a duty and motivated in part by guilt, that it must be worn like a badge on the sleeve if one is to be loved and accepted in return, that it can be withdrawn all too readily by others, and that it brings anxiety and insecurity rather than joy.

The love the child will one day give to others – including one day to a partner and to children of his or her own – is akin to a plant that must be fed and nurtured during the childhood and adolescent years. The breakdown of so many adult relationships can be traced back to the experiences of childhood, and to the sad fact that those concerned were not allowed to learn the true nature of the most important of all human emotions.

In learning how to love others, children learn also how to love themselves. Love is not complete unless it can flow in both directions, inwards as well as outwards. Unless we learn to love others unselfishly and unconditionally, our love for ourselves will always be tinged with a critical lack of self-acceptance, or with some over-possessive, self-gratifying, self-centred attitude. Similarly, unless we learn to love ourselves, our love for others will always be mixed with a degree of grasping and of over-dependence, since we will look to them to compensate for the deficiencies we imagine are present always in ourselves.

Once again, the ability to love ourselves depends to a large measure upon the growth of trust, for we must learn to trust ourselves as well as to trust others. It also depends upon the growth of autonomy and competence, the feeling that, albeit with due humility, we have a right to be who we are, and to find our space and our authenticity within the world, just as others also have this right. To love ourselves depends in addition upon self-esteem, the awareness that for all our weaknesses we are trying in a valid and appropriate way to make the best of our lives. This has nothing to do with conceit – in fact in many ways it is the very opposite of conceit, since conceit stems from a basic insecurity about ourselves that drives us always into telling others what a good and important person we are. Whenever a psychologist sees excessive conceit, he or she knows that under the façade, perhaps as yet unacknowledged, there lurks an uncertain and fearful personality.

The ability to love ourselves comes primarily from a relationship with parents who are wise and mature in their own love for us, who cherish and enjoy us in childhood for what we are, and who influence our development not by trying to force us into a mould of their own making, but by giving us through their actions and their words an initiation into the true spirit of love itself.

SEXUALITY

Sexuality is one of the strongest of our innate drives. Sigmund Freud in fact saw it as the most powerful drive of all, and considered that the way in which it is allowed to develop and express itself during the formative early years determines in large measure the shape of the personality in adult life. For Freud, sexual energy is the instinctive urge to preserve the species, an urge that runs in parallel with the instinctive urge towards self-preservation. Freud identified the sex urge as emerging in children as a series of pleasurable physical sensations associated in turn with each of the so-called erogenous zones. In the first year of life (termed by Freud the oral stage of development) the erogenous zone is the mouth, followed in the second year (the anal stage) by the anus, and from the third to the seventh year (the genital stage) by the genitals. From the very first, the reactions of parents determine whether the child's sexuality develops in a psychologically adaptive or maladaptive way. Problems respectively over weaning and over toilet training result in difficulties in maturing from the oral and anal stages, while disapproval or punishment during the genital stage (where the child discovers and plays with the genitals), may condition the child into permanently associating this area of the body with guilt and disgust.

For Freud, failure to mature successfully through these three early stages of development is the prime cause of neurosis and of other psychological problems later in life. For example, weaning a child too abruptly while he or she is still gaining erogenous pleasure from sucking will prevent him or her from passing naturally from the oral phase. The result will be not only that sexual pleasure might in later years still be associated primarily with the mouth, but that certain personality traits will also be unnaturally 'oral'. The individual concerned thus might be excessively gullible (ready to swallow anything), or given to verbal aggression (biting sarcasm for example). Over-strict toilet training will prevent the child from maturing naturally out of the anal phase, with consequences for the personality that might involve meanness (refusal to give anything away) or explosive rage (inability to control the emotions). Punishment and guilt for touching the genitals will prevent the child from maturing from the genital stage, leading dependent upon temperament to frigidity on the one hand or to unbridled sexuality on the other.

Few psychologists take Freud's sexual stages of development very literally any longer, but there is no doubt that two of his general theories of infantile sexuality are considered of great importance. The first is that the reactions of adults towards young children's sexuality can influence their life-long ability to handle sex in mature and psychologically healthy ways, and the second is that repression or warping of the sex drive during these early years can contribute towards neuroses and other psychological problems both in childhood and in the future.

Sex education is therefore something that must be approached with great sensitivity by adults. Children have no idea that there is anything 'wrong' in the pleasure they obtain from their erogenous zones in the early years of life. If therefore they are deprived of this pleasure or punished for it, they naturally experience great confusion. The message they receive is that there is something 'sinful' about certain parts of their own bodies, and something 'sinful' about taking pleasure from these parts. So powerful is this confusion that even when the child is an adult and able to approach things rationally, it may still persist at an unconscious level, leading not only to doubts and perhaps disgust over one's sexuality but also to a wider uncertainty over the validity of the whole of one's emotional life.

The best sex education is one that starts at an early age, so that the child learns the facts of sexual life as naturally as facts about other areas. The secret is to answer the child's questions about sexuality openly and truthfully as they occur. As early as the third year of life many children will already be wanting to know where babies come from, and will already be showing great curiosity both about their own bodies and about the bodies of others. An absence of prudery within the home is essential during these years if children are to learn that there is nothing about the human body of which we should be ashamed, and the earlier their curiosity is satisfied, the less insistent and potentially embarrassing this curiosity is likely to become. Children need to know that male and female bodies are made differently, and why. They need to know where babies come from, and how they are conceived in the first place. This is part of their natural interest in the world around them, and it is only the awkwardness of adults in answering these questions that gives a child the idea that interest in the body and in sexuality is somehow different and less wholesome than interest in other things.

Children also need to know that sexuality is at its most life-enhancing when it is part of a loving relationship, and need to know that as an expression of love it is joyful and liberating. As they grow older, they also need to know that many people misunderstand and misuse sexuality, just as they misunderstand and misuse every other important aspect of being human, and that in consequence there are certain safeguards and standards that need to be observed. But these can be imparted to children sensibly and openly, and while instilling caution in them should certainly not be allowed to instil fear about any aspects of the sex act itself.

Just as children need honesty and openness about sex, so do they about other natural bodily functions. Freud was not the only person to notice that small children derive pleasure from evacuating their bladders and bowels, and that they take a lively (and natural) interest in the results. If this interest is met with disapproval and disgust by adults, children once again experience confusion about their own bodies. On the one hand they are encouraged to perform when put on the potty, and rewarded with approval when they do, yet on the other the results of their performance are regarded as unmentionable, and flushed away before they have a chance to see what they look like. In this as in so many other things, it is vital to remember that once small children have their curiosity satisfied, they quickly lose interest and turn to other things. It is only when we (for mysterious reasons beyond their understanding) refuse to satisfy this curiosity, that it can become troublesome to both them and to us.

If we as adults find difficulty in handling children's curiosity about the body and its functions in this way, then this is a good opportunity to ask ourselves why. Are we still carrying early inappropriate conditioning about these matters ourselves? Do we equate sexuality *per se* with something sinful and dirty? Do we believe there is something unpleasant about the body and its functions? If we do identify problems in our own attitude towards these areas, then we can learn so much from our small children. Once upon a time we were as innocent and as open about these matters as they are. Whatever has gone wrong since then is clearly simply a learned reaction. If it was learned it can be unlearned, and we can free ourselves once more to see the body as a noble temple of the spirit, and see its functions as God-given and no cause for either shame or guilt.

CO-OPERATION

Co-operation stems from an ability to see that others have wishes and rights besides ourselves, and that through helping each other we are all enabled to experience life more richly. In many ways it is closely associated with self-discipline (in that it sometimes involves putting the needs of others before our own), and with love (in that it can arise naturally out of a wish to see those we love made happy).

At times it also calls upon sympathy and empathy, the former being the readiness to see that others have problems (large or small) and could do with our help, and the latter the sensitivity that allows us to feel the needs of others as keenly as if they are our own.

Co-operation, like many of the other tasks of childhood, is learned in part through example. When others co-operate with us (adults with children, children with each other) we are allowed to experience the way in which co-operation enhances social relationships and makes life more pleasant and effective. It is also learned through direct teaching. We point out the benefits of co-operation to our children, and indicate the occasions when it is most necessary. Similarly we praise and encourage children when they show co-operation, and remind them when for one reason or another they forget to co-operate in the way that they should.

Within the home, co-operation is demonstrated in a variety of ways, from one child helping another to children agreeing to follow the wishes of their parents even if these do not fit in exactly with what they themselves want to do. But perhaps it is seen to most effect in the readiness of children to take their full share in the many domestic tasks inseparable from running a home. The rule here is that the more children are encouraged and allowed to help when they are young (and when helping in the home is still seen by them as play), the more willing they will be to help in the years to come. I am constantly amazed by parents who have banned their children from the kitchen and from the workroom when the children were in the messy stage, and when every job with which they helped took twice as long as it otherwise would, and who then bemoan the fact that when their children are older and their help is wanted it is never forthcoming. Allow children to be drawn fully into the experience of helping when they are young (even to the extent of asking for their ideas and opinions whenever possible), and they will voluntarily remain part of the experience when they grow older.

It hardly needs saying that this applies just as much to boys as to girls. Where there are brothers and sisters within the family, they should both be allowed (and later expected) to help equally. And more should not be demanded of a quick, efficient child than of his or her slower siblings. Children are very quick to spot unfairness (particularly when they see themselves as victims!), and few things can be guaranteed to generate more ill-will in a child than consistently being asked to do more around the house than brothers or sisters. And no comparisons should be drawn between siblings. Some members of a family excel in some things, other members in others. But the worst possible strategy is to hold one child up as an example to his or her brothers and sisters, whether it is in terms of efficiency within the home, academic work, or matters of temperament and personality. Not only does it lead to fierce resentment towards parents in the children who come off worst in these comparisons but it can also lead to jealousy and enmity between the children concerned. As far as possible, all children should feel prized for who they are, and not come to think of themselves as part of a family pecking-order.

INHERITANCE VERSUS ENVIRONMENT

Thus far we have been discussing the learning tasks faced by the child on the path to psychological and emotional growth. But parents naturally wonder what part inheritance plays in these early years – and indeed throughout life. In other words, how much of what we are comes from our genes, and how much comes from our life experience? The answer is that both nature (inheritance) and nurture (environment) play crucial roles, and interact with each other to such an extent that it is often difficult if not impossible to separate out their relative contributions. Nature lays down the extent of our potential in all areas of psychological life, just as it lays down the potential for our physical development, and nurture decides how much of that potential is actually realized.

In terms of the learning tasks discussed in the present chapter, the most important contribution by nature is in determining what psychologists call the child's *temperament*. Temperament is effectively the raw material of personality, and research indicates that it is observable from the very early weeks of life onwards. Some babies fall into the so-called 'easy' category, in that they are adaptable, regular in their habits, sunny of disposition, and possessed of a relatively high discomfort threshold (i.e. they take minor inconveniences in their stride). Other babies come into the so-called 'difficult' category, in that they are easily disturbed by any disruption to their routine, are wary of strangers, somewhat irregular in their habits, fretful of disposition, and blessed with relatively low discomfort thresholds. By no means all babies fall into these extreme categories. Many lie somewhere between the two, and a third category consists of those who by temperament are slow to engage the world, and seem for the most part rather withdrawn and wary, and with relatively low activity levels. Yet these two extremes are a useful way of recognizing the strength of the contribution that temperament makes to the people that our children are, and indeed to the people that we ourselves are, since we all carry this raw material with us throughout life, no matter how deeply it has been influenced by our life experiences.

None of these three temperamental 'types' is better than any other, though the 'easy' children often pose parents fewer problems. They tend to be cheerful and adaptable throughout childhood, have few difficulties on starting school, and are generally popular with adults and with other children. 'Difficult' children, on the other hand, find life significantly harder. Given a more labile (readily aroused) nervous system by nature, they feel things with particular intensity, and often hover between extreme highs and lows. At times, the smallest thing may upset them, and set off floods of tears or temper tantrums. Their need is for particularly patient, consistent, and gentle but firm handling by parents. Frequent clashes of wills with mother or father only makes things worse, as children in this category are often surprisingly strong-willed and stubborn. Life, for them, is an earnest, intense business, and often they find that even the most reasonable compromise is beyond them.

Parents faced with 'difficult' children can rest assured that, given patient and understanding guidance during the important formative years, such children mature out of their negative and obstructive early behaviour, and learn how to co-operate both with themselves and with others. It is the parents of such children who also should remind themselves most frequently of the advice given elsewhere in the book, namely that it is often precisely those qualities that make a child difficult that we admire most in adults. Determination, depth of feeling, sensitivity and strength of will are the very things that make for effective, committed and compassionate adults, and it is exactly these qualities that 'difficult' children have in abundance.

A third category of child temperament identified by research, namely a wariness and a reluctance to engage fully in life, also responds well to appropriate handling by parents. In this case, the emphasis should be upon encouragement and the provision of as wide a range of stimuli as possible, rather than upon attempts to force the child to participate against his or her will. Children in this category are often naturally shy and perhaps a little timid, and can be less curious and inquisitive about life than others. Pushing them into experiences against their will often exacerbates their difficulties.

In all matters of temperament, the important thing is to recognize that children are who they are, and not who ideally we might wish them to be. They do not choose their temperaments, and often they suffer far more from any problems thus caused than do we as their parents. No child is born with a wish to make life difficult for him- or herself or for others, and many parent–child difficulties result more from misunderstandings than from anything else. The parent sees the child as being deliberately obstructive and obstinate, whereas the truth is that the child is in the grip of emotions that as yet he or she cannot control or even understand. Similarly the child sees the parent as being deliberately authoritarian and repressive, while in truth the parent is simply reacting to his or her own frustrations and worries over the child.

Patience and understanding are not easy to come by when we are engaged in tussles with seemingly intransigent small children who seem intent on nothing other than getting their own way, yet patience and understanding are amply repaid in the years ahead. All too often I have talked to parents who have become locked into a syndrome of escalating argument and counter-argument with their children, and who desperately want to find a way back to sanity and harmony. That way lies in an understanding of the inner life of the child. He or she does not yet have the maturity to appreciate fully the position of others, or to recognize their motives, or to have proper control over the powerful temperamental impulses that arise within his or her own being. Adults are far better able to exercise patience and clear-sightedness than children, and even when the going is at its most difficult, they can comfort themselves with the knowledge that appropriate parenting now will save much future anguish and distress.

AUTHORITY AND DISCIPLINE

We now need to turn to the question of how parents should deal with unwanted behaviour in children, in other words what forms of discipline or punishment they should use. Throughout the book I stress the positive aspects of good parenting, but there are times when children, being children and anxious to assert their own wishes and to test the limits of what is allowed and what is not allowed, disobey or otherwise offend against the standards that parents are trying to apply within the home. In face of this, what actions should parents most properly take?

It is axiomatic that no discipline (to use this rather harsh word in the absence of a better) is much good unless it is consistently applied. Evidence shows that children who get on well with their parents and who have the most secure sense of self-identity and self-worth praise their parents' fairness. Fairness means that a child always has a very good idea where he or she stands with parents, and knows what is allowed and what is not allowed. Furthermore, he or she knows that what is allowed and not allowed are reasonable and justified, and subject to debate, explanation, and modification by parents where appropriate.

As the last sentence suggests, such children also feel confident that they can raise issues with parents, that they will be given a proper hearing and allowed to have their say, and that wherever possible a reasonable degree of domestic democracy will be allowed. Similarly they are confident that an openness exists that allows them to express feelings, even when these involve anger towards parents. An honest parent–child relationship is never likely to develop if the child is made to feel that a guard must always be placed upon what is said for fear of giving offence. With our friends or partners we value openness of this kind, and although a child should certainly be guided as to the most appropriate way to express feelings or a point of view, this should not extend to a blanket censorship of all genuine expressions of emotion or of opinion.

To this we can add that children who get on well with their parents are usually confident that when upsets do arise, these will be over quickly and never allowed to menace the parent–child relationship. One of the most damaging forms of discipline possible is that in which parents threaten to withdraw their love from the child who is considered to have misbehaved, or when they remain cold to him or her for hours or days and force the child to feel that, like household gods, they must be appeased by a long sacrifice of extra-good behaviour. Few things could be better calculated to make a child feel insecure and rejected, and in later life to experience resentment and bitterness towards the parents concerned.

A satisfactory disciplinary relationship should be based primarily upon respect and understanding. The child respects his or her parents, and understands the reason for their expectations, even if at times these prove inconvenient or even actively unwelcome. In such a relationship, the most effective sanction against unwanted child behaviours is simply withdrawal of approval from them. If we respect and value others, then we care what they think about our actions, and it matters very much to the child that parents should like what he or she happens to do. If the withdrawal of approval is accompanied by an explanation, so much the better, but in every event it should be supplemented by guidance on how things can be put right. In any case, emphasis on what is wanted rather than upon what is unwanted is always more effective – 'put your toys away' rather than 'don't leave things in a mess', 'do it quietly' rather than 'don't make so much noise', 'take turns' rather than 'don't be selfish'. And as emphasized in Chapter 3, any critical labels should always be directed towards the child's behaviour rather than towards the child him- or herself.

THE LAW OF NATURAL CONSEQUENCES

Whenever withdrawal of approval together with guidance as to the required behaviours are insufficient, the most effective sanction is what is known as *the law of natural consequences*, i.e. the application of the 'law' that we learn best if we are allowed to experience the consequences or outcomes of our actions. Thus if a child is needlessly rough with a toy and breaks it, he or she has to do without it for a reasonable time before it is mended or replaced. The child who leaves food at table experiences hunger before the next meal (by far the best way, incidentally, to deal with feeding problems) and so on. The child who does not leave for school when asked to do so arrives late and experiences the problems that this creates. And so on.

The law of natural consequences obviously can't be allowed to operate if it involves any physical risk to the child, and in any case the law is sometimes inappropriate because the consequences concerned will not become immediately apparent. Nevertheless, whenever suitable, it is the most telling and intelligent form of sanction. It should never be presented to the child as a form of adult punishment. It is solely a way of helping the child recognize the links between cause and effect. Knowledge of these links helps us weigh our actions more carefully, to think ahead when necessary, and to realize that in many instances we are the architects of our own life-experiences. Children should be warned of the consequences of their actions at the time, and if they persist in the behaviours concerned, reminded when the consequences arrive that they themselves are responsible for these results.

CORPORAL PUNISHMENT IN THE HOME

In any discussion of discipline within the home, the question of corporal punishment usually arises. Should children be smacked? And can a smack be interpreted as a 'natural consequence', provided the child is warned in advance that it will follow the misdemeanours concerned? The answer is that corporal punishment teaches the child that it is acceptable – even desirable – that big people should hit small people in order to get what they want. And further that if the small person should dare to try and hit back in self-defence, he or she will call down even greater vengeance from on high. Clearly this is not the kind of lesson that any of us, on reflection, would want to teach.

As to natural consequences, there is no connection at all in the sense intended by the parent. In fact corporal punishment may serve seriously to blur the child's recognition of the law. He or she now feels upset (and perhaps resentful and hostile) because of the smack, and may lose sight altogether of the reasons why the original action was an unwise one. Corporal punishment may indeed invoke the law of natural consequences, but in a way very different from the parent's wishes. The natural consequence of corporal punishment is that it places the relationship between parent and child under severe threat. The parent has failed to honour and respect the vulnerability (physical and psychological) of the child, or to honour and respect his or her real feelings for the child. And the child now finds it harder to honour and respect the authority of the adult, since that authority now seems to be based upon the infliction of pain and fear rather than upon love and explanation.

It must be accepted that adults are sometimes driven to the limits by the seeming intransigence of the small child, and may hit out simply as a way of relieving their anger and frustration. This is human and perhaps understandable, but it has nothing to do with the most effective way of raising a child, and we must never be beguiled into thinking that it does. Many parents often confess to extreme feelings of guilt after striking their children, and although on these occasions they must make due allowances for their mood of the time, these feelings accurately represent their understanding of the relationship they know should exist between them and their child.

PARENTAL DISCIPLINARY STYLES

It is useful at this point to refer to the four general *styles* of parental discipline identified by psychological research. These styles do not of course cover parents who are violent and abusive towards their children. They represent instead the four broad categories into which the great majority of normal, caring, well-meaning parents fall. The four categories and their descriptions, together with the child behaviours that research shows characteristically result from them, are given below.

PARENTAL STYLES AND RESULTING CHILD BEHAVIOURS

Parental Style	Child Behaviours
Authoritative Expect children to behave intellectually and socially at levels consistent with age and abilities. Warm, nurturing, solicit children's opinions and feelings. Give explanations for decisions.	Independent, self-assertive, friendly with peers, co-operative with parents, happy, achievement-motivated, successful.

Authoritarian	
Assert power and control without warmth or two-way communication. Set absolute standards. Demand obedience, respect for authority and tradition, and hard work.	Tendency to social withdrawal. Lacking in spontaneity. Girls dependent and lacking in achievement motivation. Boys tending to be aggressive towards peers.
Indulgent	
Make few demands of children. Accepting, responsive and child-centred.	Positive and vital in mood, but immature and lacking in impulse control, social responsibility and self-reliance. Tendency towards aggression.
Neglecting	
Preoccupied with own activities, uninvolved with children, and uninterested in their activities. Avoid two-way communication, and take little notice of children's opinions or feelings.	Tendency towards moodiness and lack of concentration. Profligate, low impulse and emotional control. Little interest in schooling. High truancy rates and drug-taking.

Some parents will fluctuate in their parental styles, dependent upon external circumstances and even upon the mood of the moment. Other parents may fall somewhere between two or more of the categories. Nevertheless, these four styles and the results they each produce provide valuable practical guidance on the best way to discipline children if we wish them to grow into happy, well-adjusted and sociable people.

SINGLE PARENTS

As made clear in the Introduction, I am taking as my model the two-parent family, and stressing that all the information in the book can be adapted to fit individual circumstances. However, it is important at the end of these two chapters on the tasks of childhood to make some reference to single-parent families and their particular challenges. In the single-parent family one parent – 90 per cent of the time the mother – has to fulfil the role of both mother and father. Inevitably this puts extra pressures upon the budget, and upon parental time and energy. In addition, the single parent lacks the close emotional support of the second parent, not only at the personal level but at the level of disciplining and guiding the children, and of making necessary decisions about them and their lives.

A good single-parent family is very much better for the child than a mediocre two-parent one, but single-parent children do lack the role-model of the good second parent (of whatever sex). Where the missing parent is a father, this can be particularly difficult for boys, who may in consequence be unsure of their manhood, and may (dependent upon temperament) react either by becoming exaggeratedly macho, or by emphasizing the gentler, more feminine side of their natures. The first reaction can cause problems for mothers, and the second can cause problems for the child. A son who follows the exaggeratedly masculine path can become unruly, aggressive, disobedient and troublesome, both inside and outside the home. A son who emphasizes the more feminine side of his nature can be picked on and bullied by other boys (particularly if they too feel the need to assert their manhood).

Girls of course will also suffer from the absence of a father, both for emotional reasons and because the parent of the opposite sex plays some part in establishing the child's role model. But girls suffer particularly from the absence of a mother since, as with a boy and his father, the mother is the main source of the feminine role model. In the absence of a mother, a girl may also have to take an unfair share of the domestic chores. Yet girls are generally more socially and psychologically sensitive than boys. They are more aware of other people and their needs, and at the same time more in touch with their own feelings. In addition (although girls can bully each other unmercifully at times), a girl stands a better chance of being supported by her friends, and of learning a satisfactory feminine role from them.

In the absence of a mother, boys may not only lack a nurturing, feminine influence in their lives, they may have difficulty in learning how to relate appropriately to women. They may either have an idealized picture of them, or adopt an exploitive and uncaring attitude towards them. Neither extreme is likely to help prepare the way for a mutually satisfying partnership in adult life.

Another problem sometimes faced by children in single-parent families is demands from their parent for the emotional support which should by rights be given by an adult partner. This is a danger in any family, as made clear elsewhere, but obviously the risk is greater where there is only one parent present. The reverse scenario is also a problem. A single parent may find a child making demands for time and attention that should by rights be made of a second parent.

Further challenges can arise if the absent second parent has access to the child. Where such an arrangement works well it benefits all concerned, but sometimes it leads to conflicts of loyalty for the child, and at others to invidious comparisons between the first parent (who provides all the daily support for the child) and the second (who provides fun on the weekends). Related challenges can be posed by grandparents if they also battle for the child's loyalties.

There are no easy answers to any of these problems, but to recognize their existence is an essential first step. In the case of role models, uncles and aunts (or suitable friends of the opposite sex) can often help, and attempts should be made to see that children have as much contact with them as possible. And as far as emotional demands are concerned, the rule is not to expect from a child what can only be given by another adult. This is often difficult, especially for parents who feel otherwise lonely and isolated, but if children are expected to provide a form of support which they are not yet mature enough to give (and which in any case belongs to a relationship between grown-ups and not between parent and child), they can become emotionally confused, their emotional development is disrupted, and they fall prey to guilt and self-doubt at their inability to produce what is demanded of them.

When it comes to meeting the child's own needs for time and attention, the helpful rule (just as with two-parent families) is that children who are confident they can have adult attention whenever it is needed (or confident that the attention will be given the moment the adult is free) are not the ones who become over-demanding. It is the insecure child, and the child who has learned that pestering and nagging are the only ways to get attention, who causes the problems. So giving attention, even when we feel least like it, is the only way of ensuring that a child will increasingly come to respect the times when we are tired or busy, and voluntarily postpone their requests until later. It is also as well to remember that no amount of consumer goods (toys, television, videos and the like) can ever substitute in the child's mind for the attention of a sympathetic adult. It is through this attention that children are reassured that they are loved, that they are interesting people to be with, and that above all they are human beings and not machines.

The problem of a child's divided loyalties between the single parent and the absent parent is perhaps the most difficult of all. The best solution is through the co-operation and understanding of all concerned, but there are many occasions when this unfortunately is not forthcoming. In such instances, the most helpful advice is not to blame the child. He or she has not made a conscious decision to be disloyal (unless you have shown them that this is an effective weapon to use against you!). They may be just as confused and unhappy about it all as you are, even though they hide it effectively (children can quickly become artists at concealing their feelings, even from themselves). The only way forward is not to blame the child, and not to appear upset by any invidious comparisons he or she may make between you and the absent parent. The child can be reminded, briefly and in a matter-of-fact way, of the contributions you make to his or her welfare, but it is better not to attempt any comparisons with the absent parent. Don't play the game of loyalties. Actions speak far louder than words, and provided no pressures are put upon them, children are well able to conclude for themselves who is making the major contribution to their lives.

Let us not make single parenting sound too daunting though. In many single-parent families there is an especially strong bond between parent and child. Some single parents are single parents by choice. Others become single parents as a way out of impossible relationships, and as a way of giving their children and themselves a more harmonious and stable home life than they ever had as two-parent families. Others who have become single parents through tragedy work devotedly to make up for the absence of a much-loved partner. Very many single parents thus give their children far more of the precious gifts of good parenting than many sons or daughters receive from two-parent families. And deservedly, such single parents reap a double reward.

STEP-PARENTS

Step-parents face a very different set of challenges from single parents, but the challenges are very real nevertheless. Often step-parents face problems of resentment and jealousy from step-children, and feel resentment and jealousy in return. If they bring children of their own into the family, there may be rivalries and hostility between the two sets of children, and difficulties in the relationship between their own children and the other step-parent. There may be problems over the discipline and control of step-children, clashes of interests and loyalties, disputes over 'territory' within the home, and over the rules and regulations relating to it.

The best possible advice to a step-parents is not to interfere too much with any aspects of the family into which you have just come. Allow a period during which your step-children can become used to you, grow to like and trust you, and recognize that you are no threat to them or to their relationship with their natural parent. Don't try to impose your child-rearing ideas upon your new family. Everybody needs a period of re-adjustment and re-orientation. And, above all, don't allow yourself to be jealous of the attention your step-children ask of their natural parent. The children were there before you, and they have their rights.

Once you are fully accepted as a family member, you have, of course, more scope for making your views felt, but it is important to remember that you must never exceed your authority. As a step-parent, you rely upon the continuing acceptance of your new family. The parental 'contract' of a step-parent is rather different from that of a natural parent, however close the ties between you and your step-children become. There are times when it may be necessary to keep silent when you wish to speak, and times when it is better not to give advice than to give it. But with a sensitivity to what is appropriate and what is not, step-parenting can become a particularly rewarding and beneficial relationship for all concerned. Many children come to love and respect a step-parent as much as any natural parent, and many a step-parent gives their step-children love and care to match any given by natural mothers or fathers.

ADOPTIVE PARENTS

There is little specific that needs to be said about adoptive parents, since all the evidence shows that the bond within good adoptive families is every bit as strong as that within natural families. There is nothing special about the blood tie (after all, fathers and mothers normally have no blood tie between them), and the quality of love between adopted children and their parents can be every bit as strong as that in the natural child-parent relationship. Adoptive parents are people who have a particular longing for children, and who have been through more heart-ache (and selection) before having their children than the vast majority of natural parents. They are thus likely to treasure their children in a very particular way, and to appreciate the gift of parenthood more than most.

The evidence shows that children from adoptive homes tend to be at least as well adjusted, and on the whole to be more successful at school, than children brought up by natural parents, probably because of the extra attention and encouragement given by many adoptive parents. They do every bit as well in life, and (perhaps because they are usually adopted into very stable homes) tend to form good inter-personal relationships. The only special query that arises in adoptive families is when best to tell children of their adoption. The answer is as early as possible, at the very time when they start to ask the usual childhood questions about where babies come from. As with sex education, where honest, open details about pregnancy, intercourse, conception and the like should be given to children as soon as they want to know them, the facts of adoption should be information with which the child grows up. No small child thinks it odd (nor should they, since there is nothing remotely odd about it) to be told that some children are brought up by the parents who conceived them, while others are brought up by parents entrusted with their love and care after they were born.

Later, when they are at school, adopted children may come to feel a little 'different' from their friends for a time, since more children are brought up by their natural than by adoptive parents, but this feeling is not likely to last long. All children are 'different' from each other in one way or another (in personality, appearance, ability, background, race, religion and so on – to say nothing of the difference between two-parent, single-parent and step-parent families), and the important thing for a child is to be loved and to love. Your child will quickly come to realize that it is the quality of the family that is important, and not the way in which it was put together. As to whether other people should be told about the adoption (supposing for example you move to another part of the country), this is entirely up to you and your children. It is your own business first and foremost, and like the rest of your own business, it is up to you to decide who to share it with.

CHAPTER 5

The Child as Scientist

THE DOMINANCE AND LIMITATIONS OF SCIENCE

In the West we live in a world dominated increasingly by science. Science gives rise to the technology that produces the goods without which we have come to regard life as impossible. But more than this, science presents us with a picture of how the world works. It explains reality to us, offers laws to account for its processes, and even claims to answer questions as to the ultimate origin of life, the existence or otherwise of a soul, and our fate after death.

Yet for all its power and its usefulness, science is only a partial way of looking at the world. It is a science of material things, of the objective reality 'out there'. The inner world of the mind, of thoughts, ideas, creativity, and of feelings and emotions is barely touched by it. True we have a science of psychology that is very effective and helpful in describing these inner qualities, in observing their influence upon outer behaviour, in assessing them, in building theories to demonstrate their operation, and in measuring the physical changes in the body (brain waves, physiological reactions) that accompany them, but it is silent as to their exact nature, their origins or their purpose. Consciousness, that quality of ourselves that includes all these aspects of our inner world, remains a mystery to science. It even appears that we could have evolved and survived very satisfactorily without it. There is no evolutionary reason, as far as we know, for consciousness ever to have arisen in our long ascent through the dim aeons of our presence upon the face of the planet.

Science therefore has a limited range of convenience. Within that range, it is very good. Outside it, science speaks with no real authority. And even within it, we must remember that science is only an attempt by men and women to represent external reality in terms of theories and models. Scientific laws are not absolutes, but our way of thinking about absolutes. They are subject to change and debate, and give only one version of the external world. No one can doubt the usefulness of this version, but if we mistake it for reality itself, then we handicap our ability to question it and, in certain ways that I return to later, to go beyond it.

SCIENCE AND THE CHILD

The dilemma faced by the thoughtful adult when teaching science is how to help children understand both its strengths and its limitations. To live safely and successfully in the world they must master a vast amount of scientific information, going from the basic qualities of the objects around them to (if need be) the wonders of sub-atomic physics. Yet they must be allowed to remain sensitive to their intuitive feelings about the world, to its mystery and beauty, and to their own sense of wonder in the face of it.

On the one hand they have to learn such things as that bricks are hard objects, that water can drown, that fire can burn, that roads are dangerous, that certain things are alive while other things are not, and so on. On the other hand they have to retain their inborn awareness that what goes on inside their own consciousness is as 'real' and as important as what goes on outside it. Later, they need (if they are to achieve real understanding) to learn that the distinction between outer and inner worlds is not as hard and fast as it seems. This involves recognizing that what goes on in the mind actually 'creates' what goes on outside it. Modern science, as opposed to the over-materialistic science of the nineteenth century, accepts that all things are formed from a flow of sub-atomic energy, which is given shape and colour and substance only by the way in which we experience it. Even the most solid of objects is in reality composed almost entirely of empty space, and only appears solid since the atomic 'stuff' of which it is composed ('stuff' that is itself only a mysterious form of non-material energy) is in rapid and continuous motion.

The great scientist Sir Oliver Lodge pointed this out over 50 years ago when he wrote that:

> most of our mundane experience is illusory . . . we are surrounded by phantasmal appearances through which our senses cannot penetrate. Matter is what we primarily apprehend through the senses; but the nature of matter is mysterious.

If our senses were different, we might be able to see this strange, whirling flux of energy that lies behind the apparent solidity of the world, and thus experience a very different kind of reality. Even at a more mundane level, there are many things that can influence or actively harm us (such as radon gas and gamma rays) that we are unable to register at all with our senses. It is only our machines that tell us of their existence. And since our machines are themselves limited, it is not difficult to suppose that there are whole spectrums of existence that are unknown and untouched by us.

Even at an immediate level, we have no machines that can register thoughts (as opposed to registering the electrical activity of the brain that accompanies them). Thoughts are mental, non-material events, and science has no real idea how they are actually produced, or how a non-material event like a thought can lead to a physical event like walking. As an example, ponder the mystery of how the *mental* decision to move your arm is then translated into the *physical* action of the movement itself. The stock explanation that the thought sets off an electrical impulse that activates the nerves that activates in turn the muscles is insufficient as an answer. It offers simply a *description* of the neurophysiological processes that are set off by the thought; it does not tell us how the thought interacts with the body in order to activate these processes. The best way to become fully aware of the truth of this is to sit still for a moment, and then decide to move your arm, noting as you do how baffling the whole thing is when you ask exactly what is happening.

Now suppose for a moment you are a child, and you ask an adult the question 'How does my arm move when I want it to?' The adult will probably answer 'A message goes from your brain to your arm, and makes it move.' As a child, you suppose this answer is the correct one, because adults know more than you. So the mystery of how you move your arm ceases to be a mystery. Except that of course it does not – the mystery remains, the difference is that the adult's incomplete answer has led you to lose sight of it. What he or she should have said is 'We don't really know; in some wonderful way you do it by thinking about it.' The description of nerves and muscles and electrical messages can come afterwards, when the child is ready to understand that it *is* only a description. It should not be allowed to interfere with the child's awareness of the essential mystery of thought.

Children are natural explorers of their own minds. It is only if we indicate to them that the outer world, and its material objects and rewards, are more real and more important than the inner world, that they put this exploration to one side. Thus before responding to their deeper questions it is essential we begin to re-explore the inner world for ourselves, and recognize that much of the thinking we allow to go on there is conditioned by the answers adults gave when we ourselves were young. To break free of this conditioning we must attempt, with our children, to see the mind and the natural world stripped once more of the labels that others have assigned to them for us. Let's take an example of the way in which a concerned, conscientious, but conditioned adult might answer a typical question of a 5 year old.

Child: 'What is water?'
Adult: 'It's a mixture of two gases, hydrogen and oxygen. Two parts of hydrogen to one of oxygen.'
Child: 'What is gas?'
Adult: 'Air is a gas.'
Child: 'So water is like air?'
Adult: 'That's right. It's really only two sorts of gases put together.'

The question and answer session is closed. The child does not understand how water can be two sorts of gases put together, but he knows that if one day the teacher asks 'What is water ?', and he answers 'Two parts of hydrogen to one of oxygen', the teacher will beam and tell him how clever he is, and hold him up as an example to the rest of the class.

Young children have a natural love of water and of water play, and the appropriate answer to a 5 year old child's question 'what is water?' is to go with him or her to explore the properties of water. How does water feel as it runs through the fingers or down the body? What happens when it touches the earth, or is thrown in sparkling droplets into the sunlight? How does it behave as it tumbles past the rocks and stones in a mountain stream? What song does it sing? What are the feelings aroused in us by a lake of still water, and by the reflections in its face of trees and the broad sweep of the blue sky? What fish swim in its depths, what plants grow there, and how do the pebbles from the river bed look when brought to the surface and held wet and shining in the hands?

The hard-nosed scientist might say this is an immature way of dealing with water: it isn't science. This view is wrong. Science is about wonder and discovery, and to experience water by touching it, seeing it, listening to it, playing with it, is better science to a small child than is the ability to trot out a dull formula in a classroom. Even more to the point, it is better poetry. The child watching the sun spread a pathway of gold on the lake is seeing the outer world as the poet sees it, and as the painter and the writer see it. The child watching a tree bending in the wind, a swallow swooping from the evening sky, the moon painting the garden silver, the autumn leaves falling from the trees outside the window, is seeing the world with the eye of an artist, and feeling the artist's upsurge of creative feeling.

In these experiences, there is no boundary for the child between science and art. Nor should there be. Science and art are both products of the human mind. They arise from the same source, and are simply alternative ways of reflecting our experience of reality. There is always something of the artist about the great scientist, and something of the scientist about the great artist. The artificial separation between the two areas that we see in the twentieth century is a relatively modern invention. Back through history the artist and the scientist, if not one and the same person, had a deep respect and understanding for each other, a respect and understanding that made science more human and art a more faithful representation of the outer world.

If we return again to the young child's question about water, and the distinction between experiencing water as a living substance or as a laboratory formula, we can extend it to cover that perennial existential question 'What am I?' One way to answer it is to give once more a laboratory formula, covering this time each of the substances that together make up the human body, and adding in the electrical impulses that fire the nervous system. Another is to experience, from inside, the essence of oneself as a thinking, feeling, hoping, dreaming human being. Which of these two answers approaches more closely to the truth about yourself? They are both scientific in that they are based upon exploration and discovery, but whereas one has to do purely with chemistry and a touch of neurophysics, the other has to do with the experience of life itself.

OTHER WAYS OF MISLEADING CHILDREN

In addition to those already touched upon, there are many areas where we mislead children by our answers to their questions, thereby profoundly influencing their world-view for years to come. Space only allows a few brief examples.

Time

We live in a time-dominated world. We allow our lives to be ruled by time, and our science to be dominated by the concept of a space–time universe. Thus we condition our children into believing early that there is a reality called time that moves at the same inexorable rate from the future through the present to the past. This psychological myth of time has a marked effect upon our concept of reality. And myth it is, for in truth what we really experience is a process of change taking place around us, and we invent a concept called 'time' to explain it. Thus we grow up with a view that 'time' is the actual cause of change. The result is we become preoccupied with how old we are, and assume that age determines the state of our bodies and minds. In fact people *change* at very different rates, and it may even be that through certain exercises such as yoga the mind and body can to some extent reverse the processes of change and actually grow younger. We also become preoccupied with the days of the week and the months of the year. In fact nature recognizes no difference between one day and another. In nature there are no Sundays and Mondays, and no seven days to a week. To be conditioned into believing otherwise seriously distances us from nature and her own natural rhythms.

The mistaken notion of time also seriously limits a child's ability to understand many important scientific concepts. For instance, even most adults find it almost impossible to understand that an astronaut will, by virtue of the speed by which he or she travels through space, experience the passing of much less time than we will here on earth. A twin out in space will therefore age less than a twin brother or sister here on earth over the same period. Similarly, even adults find it hard to understand that so-called black holes out in space have a gravity so powerful that even time cannot escape from them. Thus for black holes time stands still. However, replace 'time' with the concept of change, and these ideas become much easier to understand. Travelling at vast speeds through space, the rate of change slows down. With the powerful gravity of a black hole, everything is held so tightly together that nothing can change.

History

The view of history given to the child is that it involves continuous progress by the human race. In fact, many of the greatest insights into the human condition came from men and women who lived many hundreds of years ago such as the Buddha, Socrates and Christ. In many areas of human thinking we have in fact regressed rather than progressed, and the same goes for social relationships, and indeed the quality of life in general.

Memory

The popular view of memory is that it carries a reasonably complete record of our lives. In reality, consciously at least, we remember only a minute fraction of the things that happen to us. A simple experiment such as attempting to remember the journeys you made as a child to and from school will demonstrate this to you. Yet we continually blame children for forgetting things we consider they should remember, and make no allowance for the fragmentary, illusory mystery of memory.

Miracles

Received wisdom has it that miracles are against the laws of nature, and could not possibly have happened. Even the Christian Church often takes this view. Yet if we approach miracles on the basis of evidence rather than of preconceptions, we are forced to very different conclusions. If we study the numerous eyewitness accounts by level-headed academics and journalists of the modern miracle at Fatima in Portugal for example, where, following visions of the Virgin Mary by three peasant children, a crowd of 70,000 people are said to have seen the sun change colour and then 'dance and whirl' in the sky, we are left with the clear impression that something quite extraordinary took place. At another level, the current findings of parapsychology also indicate that phenomena can take place outside the currently known laws of science.

Language

Language is a precious and vital tool, yet there are misconceptions about it that serve to distort and confuse our notions of reality itself. An example of this is the belief into which children are conditioned that providing a term for something is the same as explaining it. In addition, they are all too often taught to define things in terms of opposites. A is A they are told, because it isn't B. The result is that they acquire a fragmented, oppositional view of the world rather than a unified, holistic one. Everything is expressed in terms of 'either . . . or' rather than of 'both . . . and', a form of thinking that makes it almost impossible to understand the deep yet meaningful paradoxes at the heart of life.

Life and Death

Of all the opposites that condition consciousness, the notion given to children that life and death are in fundamental opposition is one of the most damaging. If death is the opposite of life, then death becomes the great fear. Yet in reality both the mind and the body live and die and live again in each moment. Within life there is always the presence of death. Life and death develop out of each other in a constant, never-ending process. The Eastern spiritual traditions teach that life and death are ultimately the same, two sides of the one coin and each meaningless without the other. By dissolving the artificial distinction between life and death, we are able to contemplate the latter without terror, to view each passing moment as a preparation for it. When death is recognized in this light, we become open to an understanding of its real meaning, and of the life that, in the cyclical nature of all things, arises from out of it.

Other examples, such as the importance of dreams, of myths legends and stories, and of imagination have already been dealt with or are dealt with later, as is the mistaken notion that science can answer the questions of reality. Cultural conditioning in areas such as these leads children to see the world in restricted and unhelpful ways. As Carl Jung points out, so effective a filtering system does consciousness become as a result that it leaves us deaf and blind to a vast spectrum of inner and outer experience. If we are able to free ourselves from this conditioning and expand our consciousness:

> there will be a whole sphere of knowledge and experience in which all functions, all ideas, will enter besides our ordinary consciousness.

If this process is denied, the inner voice falls silent – or rather its whispers go unheard. This was the reason why Gurdjieff, using a different metaphor, remarked that we each live in a splendid mansion, but rarely move out of the basement.

WHAT IS A GOOD TEACHER?

Discussion of how we should respond to the child's early questions and avoid the wrong kinds of cultural conditioning brings us to a more general consideration of teaching and of what makes a good teacher. The child's first teachers are his or her parents, and they remain in many ways the most important influences throughout the childhood years. As teachers, the parents initiate the child into whole swathes of knowledge. This is already evident from what I have said earlier about the vital importance of helping children accept and understand their emotions, learn social and moral behaviours, and accomplish the vital tasks of childhood (Chapters 3 and 4). But the ground covered so far in this chapter also indicates how important parents are as teachers of wisdom about the material world, and about the mind and the nature of reality.

The ways in which we as adults respond to children's questions are like the passages in a book that we are helping them to write, and which they will carry with them and refer to throughout life. The example of how to respond to the question 'What is water?' illustrates something of the way in which these passages should be written, and the kind of teacher we should try always to become.

There are in fact two distinct styles of teacher. The first is the person who teaches from an assumed position of superiority. This is the teacher who essentially says to the child 'As I know more than you, I will give you the right answers to your questions, and you must learn them carefully and say them back to me each time I ask you for them.' Such a teacher believes that he or she knows what is best for the child, and understands how the child should see the world. The teacher may be very knowledgeable and very dedicated, and may genuinely want to give children as much information as possible, and may take unselfish delight in their success in absorbing this information, and in using it to get good marks for cleverness in the eyes of the adult world.

The second style of teacher is the person who teaches from a position of humility. He or she recognizes the uniqueness of each individual, and accepts that there are different kinds of knowledge, each of them useful for a particular purpose but (like the chemical composition of water) of no relevance once we pass beyond that purpose. If such a teacher has read much philosophy, they will also know that Socrates, one of the founding-fathers of modern Western philosophy, was described by the Oracle at Delphi (i.e. the priestess of Apollo) as the wisest man in all Athens, since he was the only person wise enough to know that he knew nothing. By 'know', the Oracle was here referring to Socrates' recognition of the provisional, uncertain nature of all knowledge, and of the need constantly to keep a mind that is open and creative.

The two styles of teacher thus differ greatly in their approach to teaching. The first sees the task basically as one of transmission. What is in the teacher's head must be transmitted to the heads of children. If children fail to learn, this is because they are slow learners, or because they have not been listening carefully enough or trying hard enough. The teacher may be very sympathetic and very patient with them, but ultimately he or she regards their failures as due to their own shortage of ability or lack of application. The second teacher sees teaching as a creative process, in which the child and the teacher share together in developing what is essentially a new body of knowledge, a body of knowledge particular to each child and that represents his or her personal way of seeing and knowing the world. Such a body of knowledge is created not just from what adults transmit to children, but from a subtle blend of what adults have to offer and what the children themselves bring to the experience. Much of this knowledge will be held in common with the rest of us, but important areas of it will possess a unique quality. For no one else can look out at the world with the eyes of the individual child, or listen to it with the individual child's ears, or touch it with their hands, or experience it with their emotions. And no one else can think about it with their thoughts, or dream about it with their dreams.

For the second teacher, children's difficulties in learning are due less to their own failings than to incongruencies between the adult way of seeing the world and their way. If children are to learn, the teacher sees it as her job to bring these two ways into harmony, so that each can understand and offer its wisdom to the other. For the second teacher, we teach children not because we are superior to them, but because we are a little further along the road that all must travel. And to the second teacher, the art of teaching lies in turning back and retracing that road until we are walking beside the child, and shortening our stride so that he or she is not expected to run breathlessly to keep up with us. For the second teacher, to present to children facts and information they do not fully understand is to stay ahead of them on the road, and shout over our shoulders incomprehensible words that are carried away on the wind. It is to force them to devote all their efforts to getting within earshot of us, with no time to enjoy the scenery to right and left, or to avoid stumbling over the false markers left by those gone before.

To return to Socrates, we read in the *Phaedo* how he demonstrated to onlookers how a young uneducated slave boy could solve a complex problem in geometry if he was taken through it step by step, and allowed at each point to contribute his own thinking. It was indeed as if the boy was allowed to recall what he already knew, rather than being asked to absorb new knowledge. What Socrates showed was that true learning is always grounded in what the child brings to the task, rather than in something imposed by the adult mind. Thus true learning always starts from the familiar, from the child's own level of understanding, from where the child is at the moment, and not from where we are as adults, or from where we think the child ought to be.

By working with children in this way, we find not only that learning becomes more comprehensible to them, more alive, more exciting, more permanent, but also that in a very real sense they act in turn as *our* teacher. This becomes obvious if we go back to the example of 'What is water?' For if the child goes on with the questioning, he or she brings us face to face with the inadequacies of what we have hitherto taken for granted as a fact of life.

C: 'What is water?'
A: 'It's a mixture of two gases, hydrogen and oxygen. Two parts of hydrogen to one of oxygen.'
C: 'What's a gas?'
A: 'Air is a gas.'
C: 'What is air?'
A: 'I've just told you. It's a gas.'
C: 'Yes, but what *is* a gas?'
A: 'Well, it's a . . . well, a gas is. . . . Oh I can't explain all that to you now. Wait until you're older.'

And the chances are than when he or she is older, the child won't know what a gas is any more than the adult does, and will have to be content with the knowledge that a gas is what hydrogen and oxygen happen to be, which is the same thing as knowing that a gas is a gas. If the child studies chemistry and physics, he or she may come to know that hydrogen and oxygen each have a particular molecular structure, that molecules are made up of things called atoms, and that an atom in turn consists of a nucleus and electrons, and that the nucleus in turn consists of neutrons and positrons, and that a neutron consists of (or doesn't consist of – it depends which sub-atomic theory one happens to be reading) of things called quarks and . . . . But none of this tells us what a gas actually *is*, and as with water, we have in the end to come back to the world of the natural scientist, and of the artist and the poet and actually allow ourselves to become properly aware of gas – in the form of warm air, cold air, moving air – at a personal experiential level.

LEARNING FROM CHILDREN

By listening to the wisdom of a child's questions, we thus are helped to go back and confront once more our own questioning about the world, and to recognize again the inadequacy of the answers that we have been given and that we have come, out of habit and out of respect for popular 'science', to believe contain ultimate truth about reality.

Through this confrontation and this recognition, we are prompted to see the world in a different way, and to begin once more to question what on earth this strange and magical business of existence actually *is*. Perhaps it's natural that we should take it for granted as the years go by, but a few moments of contemplation can make us conscious once more of just how miraculous – and very odd – the fact of our existence actually is. I remember in childhood being intrigued by the fact that of all the people in the world, I happened actually to be me, and to be even more intrigued that behind this 'me' I happened to exist at all. What is it, to be alive? If you ponder this question, you find that the mind first runs through a series of sensations. To be alive is to be aware of the darkness behind the eyelids, of the sounds picked up by the ears, of the body resting against the chair and feeling the texture of clothes against the skin, of the beating of the heart, of emotions that we label 'fear' or 'anxiety' or 'excitement', of thought processes running through the mind in the form of words or of pictures. But what in fact do we mean when we speak of 'being aware' of these various stimuli? And who or what is it who is experiencing this awareness?

A few minutes spent with this exercise takes us back to the wonderment of childhood. Young children live in a state of constant questioning, and if we listen to their questions we find that they concern not only the outer world but also the very fact of being alive. 'Where did I come from?' 'Why was I born?' 'Where was I before I was born?' 'Why am I me?' 'What's it like to be you?' 'Where do we go when we sleep?' 'What happens when we die?' and so on. The questions are existential ones that arise from children's awareness of their own being, and of the deep mystery that lies at the heart of it. It is indeed strange to be alive, to be ourselves, and yet to know so little about who we are.

CHAPTER 6

The Child as Artist and Problem-Solver

ART COMES NATURALLY TO A CHILD

Just as young children are natural scientists, so they are also natural artists. As already stressed, science and art both have their source in the human mind, and both are ways in which we represent humankind's experience of reality. In the young child, curiosity and the urge to explore and find out are the bases of science, and imagination and the urge to create are the bases of the arts.

Young children are naturally creative. They have an inborn urge to draw, to paint, to model objects and people out of clay and sand, to sing, to dance, to respond to rhyme and rhythm, to reflect the world around them in conformity with their own inner vision. In all my work with young children, I have never found one who did not delight in creative expression, whether it be extroverted and outer-directed, or of the quieter, introverted kind.

Why is it, therefore, that as they grow older (and particularly as they enter adolescence) children lose this instinctive delight in artistic expression, and become, if anything, mere observers of the creativity of others? The answer is very much a cultural one. We literally teach children to stop being artists. The process begins early in childhood, when, with our utilitarian, materialistic outlook upon life we start asking children what their creations actually *mean*, or what they are *for*. To the young child, creativity is often its own end. It is the delight in doing, rather than the delight in achieving a product, that fires the child's enthusiasm. To be constantly asked to explain the purpose of the creative act quickly teaches a child that unless there is a purpose, then the activity is of no real value, and should be left behind along with other so-called childish things.

Many parents comment that their children will spend a long stretch of time absorbed in a creative activity, and then leave the task half-finished, or complete it only to show no interest in the end product. Even in a highly practical activity such as cooking, the child will enthusiastically knead pastry and add ingredients and mix and mess endlessly, yet ignore or actively reject the goodies concerned when they finally emerge from the oven. Baffling as this behaviour seems to parents, to the child it makes perfect sense. The fun is in the making, and in his or her mind there is little or no real connection between this making and the food that finally arrives on the table.

The secret therefore is to allow young children to engage in the sheer joy of the creative task, without demanding an adult response to the end-product, or an adult determination to finish the job even when the interest has gone (adult artists worth their salt are in any case constantly putting work to one side and starting all over again, constantly experimenting, trying out, rejecting, re-doing, much like children).

INHIBITING ARTISTIC INTERESTS

The process of educating children not to be artists continues when, with our preoccupation with end-products, we start passing judgement upon children's creative endeavours. We compare one child with the next, we give marks and grades, we pass comments, we show our disapproval. Each of these responses attracts attention away from the delight of creativity itself, and offers instead goals to be reached and standards to be attained. Children can certainly be helped and guided to develop their talents, but only against a background of acceptance and encouragement. It is deeply disappointing to hear children start to confess that they 'can't draw' or 'can't sing' or 'can't paint' or can't do a host of other creative acts. Everyone who can hold a pencil can draw, and everyone who can make sounds can sing. A negative view of one's own creative abilities only arises in response to the judgements of others, judgements that miss the point that the value of art lies in large measure in the deep fulfilment it gives to the artist. With our natural urge to create, we humans are only psychologically whole if we are creating. Creative activity is relaxing, therapeutic, and a vivid token of our humanity. It is one of the things that sets us apart from other species, and one of the things that produces our civilization. Through art we can express our emotions, our unique world-view, our relationship with our fellows, our spiritual longings. Without art, a large part of our birthright goes to waste.

Peoples who live close to nature have never lost sight of this fact. Dance, song, ritual drama, body painting are loved as much by adults as by children, and when engaged in socially help to hold the community together and give opportunities to each of its members to communicate feelings and share emotions. Without art, we cut ourselves off from each other, and lose ourselves in alienation and in a breakdown of the natural forces of social control.

The secret therefore is not to crush the child's creativity under the weight of adult judgement. Children are best helped to develop their sense of standards by being exposed to as much art in their environment as possible, and by being presented with the materials through which they can express their own vision, and the encouragement to believe in their own creative process. Importantly, this lack of unnecessary judgement should stretch also to the highly talented child. There is a natural tendency in adults to think of the gifted child musician or dancer as heading for a professional career in the area concerned, yet all too often this is a mistake. It is once again to place art in a utilitarian context. If the child is gifted, then we assume he or she will want to make a living out of it. But the reality may well be that the child sees art as serving another part of life than the professional. He or she may want always to keep it as its own end, as a means of refreshment and renewal, and not as a means of earning a salary.

A third mistake we often make (especially within formal education) is to demonstrate to children that we value the creative arts less than the other subjects in the school curriculum. Particularly from the early years in the secondary school, the child is given the impression that painting, drama, pottery, even poetry are fringe subjects, there for the less able, or because the unfortunate teachers of these disciplines must be employed somewhere, but of far less importance than the 'serious' subjects such as science, mathematics, technology, languages, and even social studies. Taking their cue from their teachers, it is small wonder that children begin to look down upon the creative arts as poor relations, and in many cases drop them for examination purposes at the earliest opportunity.

Thus, sadly, one of the mainstays of psychological health, of emotional expression, of social coherence disappears from our children's lives, and we are left to bemoan the increasing alienation, purposelessness, and materiality of the young.

THE MEANING OF CREATIVITY

This emphasis upon the creative arts must not allow us to forget that creativity is important in other areas of life as well. Great scientists are highly creative in their approach to their subject. Good parents are creative in their approach to parenting and to homemaking. Each of us is creative when we choose new clothes or lay out a garden or decide where and how to spend our holidays. Psychologists recognize that in addition to imagination (which is discussed fully in Chapter 8), creativity is evidenced by three main qualities, namely *fluency*, *flexibility* and *originality*. Fluency refers to the number of ideas that the creative person is able to come up with, flexibility to the extent to which they can adapt to new circumstances and new challenges, and originality to the extent to which their ideas are fresh and novel. Highly creative people tend to be high on all three of these measures, though some may excel particularly on only one or two of them.

Fluency is encouraged in children and in ourselves by allowing the free flow of ideas from the unconscious to enter the conscious mind. Usually fear of failure or of ridicule has a powerfully inhibiting effect upon this flow. Many of our best ideas, quite literally, are never allowed to see the light of day. Initially this fear comes from the reactions of others, but all too soon we take over their attitudes and start the internal process of judgement and rejection that eventually cripples our creative energies. In management training and planning, one of the most productive activities is know as *brain-storming*. During this process, the members of a management group together confront a problem by contributing all the solutions, no matter how seemingly outlandish and impractical, that come into their heads. The atmosphere is totally non-judgemental and accepting. Later, when the session is finished, the group go back over the ideas that have surfaced and identify the most promising. What has happened is that by removing censorship and the desire to come up only with the 'right' answers, individuals have been allowed to contact the inspirational source that gives rise to new ideas. These ideas are then available for scrutiny and selection and refinement by the conscious, rational mind.

The second aspect of creativity, *flexibility*, is encouraged by letting the mind move out of one-track thinking and realize that when one way forward is blocked, there are other paths that can be followed. For example, when assembling a piece of furniture or machinery from written instructions, we may reach a frustrating impasse. The thing won't come together however hard we try, and in frustration we vilify the manufacturers and the writer of the instructions. However, suddenly we begin to think flexibly, and realize that the problem is of our own making. We have been holding our would-be construction the wrong way round. We made a false assumption right at the outset, and treated the top as the bottom, or vice versa. Once we correct this assumption, everything falls into place with no more trouble.

Flexibility is the ability to see different ways of tackling old problems, to think laterally (as it is sometimes called) rather than sequentially, to recognize that existing objects or ideas can be put to alternative uses, to tolerate ambiguity in a situation rather than to be happy only if everything is straightforward and readily explicable. The good parent allows children where feasible to try to do things in their own way, to work out their own methods, instead of always rushing in with their own prepared solutions. Fluency alone may give us many new ideas, but all going in the one direction. Flexibility allows us to strike out into new territory.

The third aspect of creativity, *originality*, is characterized by the ability to come up with ideas that are novel and fresh in themselves, and to make new discoveries or propose new theories. Originality is best helped in children by recognizing that many of their ideas are original *for them*. No matter how many people have thought of the same thing in the past, for the child it is an exciting first. Originality thrives upon encouragement and recognition. All too often adults look at a child's ideas, and with the intention of being helpful point out how much better the same ideas have been proposed by someone else in the past. Faced with this unfavourable comparison, the child relegates his or her own insights to insignificance, and tries instead to take over, ready-made, those of other people.

To be truly productive, creativity must be guided, directed, and subjected to the necessary hard work and self-discipline. But there is a world of difference between initiating the child into making use of creative ideas, and inhibiting the production of these ideas in the first place. The wise parent allows creativity to come to the surface in the child, welcomes and respects it, and only then prompts the child to look for ways of developing and improving upon his or her original vision. This prompting is done primarily by questioning and inviting ('What else do you think you could do to it?', 'How do you think you could extend/improve/expand upon/make use of this?' 'Let's see if you can give it more colour/make it stronger/get it to look more life-like') rather than by telling and instructing ('Now put more colour here', 'Rub that bit out and start again', 'Use thinner/thicker/longer lines').

One of the best ways of re-creating our own creative energies as adults is to watch our children, and to allow ourselves the same spontaneity and the same joy in drawing, painting, making music or whatever. By dropping our severe self-judgements, and enjoying and valuing the creative experience for itself, we are able to enter the world of the creative artist. Whether we compare with the great painters or poets or musicians of the past is of no importance. What matters is that in creating we are experiencing the same process that they experienced, and freeing the same part of our psychological lives. In no time, we may even hear our children say how much they like what we are doing, which is reward enough for anyone.

INTELLIGENCE

Creativity is a form of problem-solving. We have the urge to represent outer reality or inner feelings in the form of a poem or a painting or a piece of music. How are we to do it? Or we have a practical difficulty to sort out, or a puzzle to solve, or a scientific challenge to meet. How are we to proceed? But there is another form of problem-solving, this time associated not with creativity but with intelligence.

Of all the areas covered by modern psychology, the concept of intelligence is probably the most influential – and perhaps the most misleading. Most people have the impression that 'intelligence' is a fixed ability, as objective and as measurable as our height or our weight. Few things could be further from the truth. Intelligence is simply a term we give to certain kinds of behaviour, in particular behaviour that involves solving problems to which there are only single right answers. Intelligence tests are no more than written examples of problems of this kind, and the score (sometimes referred to as the 'Intelligence Quotient' or 'IQ' of the person concerned) obtained on these tests is no more and no less than the individual's ability to solve these paper and pencil examples. We assume that this score tells us something about his or her capacity for solving real problems in the outside world, but since the intelligence test can only reflect a narrow range of such problems (typically those associated with verbal concepts on the one hand and mathematical and spatial on the other), the score can give us at best only a partial picture of the abilities of the person concerned.

It tells us nothing for example about the ability to solve problems in human relationships and leadership, it tells us nothing about the ethics that we bring to problem-solving, nothing about our determination and perseverance in the face of difficulties, or about our courage and our motivation. It tells us nothing about the practical strategies that individuals develop for coping with problems in business and commerce or on the shop floor, nothing about the inhibitions and anxieties that often prevent people from thinking clearly in a crisis, nothing about the self-belief often required to put our solutions into practice, and nothing about the different approaches to problem-solving favoured by people from different social and cultural backgrounds.

In short, the intelligence test is only a measure of certain kinds of rational, linear thinking. This kind of thinking is sometimes described as convergent thinking, a form of thinking in which the mind is asked to converge upon the single right answer predetermined by the person who devised the test. As such it can be contrasted with the so-called *divergent* thinking that is a feature of creativity, and that allows the mind to throw up a range of solutions to problems for which there is no single right answer.

IMPROVING INTELLIGENCE

Parents sometimes ask whether intelligence, as measured by our intelligence tests, can be improved, or whether it is decided for us by our genes. The answer is that our genes determine our potential for all kinds of thinking, and this potential seems to vary from individual to individual; nevertheless learning plays a major part in deciding the extent to which this potential is actually developed. In the case of intelligence, practice on the kind of problems contained in intelligence tests rarely produces any very dramatic improvement, principally because most children already receive from their schooling enough of the stimulation necessary for the development of whatever potential they possess in the area concerned.

As already made clear, this area is only one among many

however, and the role of the parent is to provide the child with as many opportunities as possible for discussing and analysing the wide range of issues and problems that life is likely to place in the path, and to encourage him or her to advance a point of view about them and to think of possible solutions. The child is thus helped to identify the relevant variables in any situation, to distinguish what is relevant from what is irrelevant, and to decide what is practical and what is impractical.

Much of the problem-solving that we find ourselves undertaking in life is the result of practice and of experience. We speak of getting the hang of things, of learning the ropes, yet all too often children are given a narrow education that leaves them ill-equipped for facing the challenges that await them in the outside world. Parents who talk to their children, who answer their questions, who take them on outings and prompt them to use their eyes and their ears, who buy them books and puzzles, and who explain the reasons for their own decisions in appropriate language, are doing all they can to develop the problem-solving abilities of their children and to initiate them into the habits of thinking and of enquiry that they will need if they are to make full use of their inborn potential.

THE SPECIAL CHILD

All children are individuals, and all have their own particular needs. In this sense all children are special. But the term is usually reserved for those who have needs that are somewhat out of the ordinary. Usually these needs are associated either with children who are particularly forward in one or more areas of learning and development, or who are experiencing particular problems in one or more areas. Before looking at these separate sets of needs and how they affect parents, it must be understood, however, that all children are children first, with the basic needs of children for unconditional love, environmental stimulation, play, friendship and emotional acceptance, and for help and encouragement in learning the tasks of childhood covered in Chapters 3 and 4. Their special needs can only be effectively catered for against this understanding.

Children who are unusually forward in one or more areas are often referred to as *gifted children*, and although this term is misleading (all children are gifted in their own way) I propose to use it for the sake of convenience. Children who experience particular problems with certain kinds of learning used to be called educationally subnormal (a pejorative term which has happily fallen into disuse), and are now usually referred to simply as children with learning difficulties. Let us look first at gifted children.

Gifted Children

Some children (the number is variously put at between 1 and 5 per cent of the population, though where to draw the line is largely a matter of opinion) show from an early age a precocious talent either in the fields associated with creativity or in those associated with intelligence (sometimes both). Or they may show particular physical or sporting abilities. Often – though by no means always – these talents persist across the years, and the gifted child may mature into the gifted adult. However, much may depend upon the way in which such talents are nurtured and encouraged. And here difficulties can arise, because both in the home and the school the gifted child may be misunderstood and isolated and marginalized on the one hand, or recognized and pushed too hard on the other.

Misunderstandings can come about because of the unusual nature of the child's behaviour and thinking. He or she may show striking originality, for example, and always want to do things in an individual and highly inventive and unusual way. Or the speed of their thinking and their readiness to argue and debate and contradict may be seen by adults as a threat to their authority. Unless these misunderstandings are corrected, the child may not receive an education commensurate with his or her abilities, and may in consequence become bored, disaffected, and either depressed and withdrawn or something of a trouble-maker. To make matters worse, he or she may be unpopular with children of the same age, largely through major disparities in ability and in interests. There are also dangers that gifted children may develop unsatisfactory self-images, seeing themselves either as unlikeable or as a cut above the rest of humanity.

The gifted child thus needs early diagnosis and appropriate support, and at the same time help in mixing with other children (sometimes this may mean making friends primarily with those who are somewhat older). *Emotionally* they will usually be no older than their years, whatever their other abilities, and they will need help in coming to terms with their gifts, in seeing themselves as basically neither different nor superior to other children, and in enjoying being children and the things of childhood rather than trying to become premature adults. Wherever their talents lie – music, mathematics, art, languages, science, swimming, gymnastics or whatever – they are likely to need extra help from experts, and perhaps an extra commitment of time and money from parents (together with understanding and sympathetic teachers at school), but it is important that all concerned centre themselves in the present and not in the future. Parents who feel that they are 'investing' a great deal in their child, and who expect a 'return' in the future, are putting far too much pressure upon him or her. In the end, it is the children themselves who must eventually decide whether to go on and develop the talents concerned at a professional level. In many cases they will decide that their interests ultimately lie elsewhere, and in others they may simply lose something of their early giftedness.

The Child with Learning Difficulties

We all have learning difficulties in some areas. Problems only arise when these areas include the so-called basic subjects of reading, writing and mathematics. Something like 20 per cent of children have real difficulties in these areas at some time or other during their school careers, and it is the job of the school to have these difficulties diagnosed by experts from the school psychological service, and to provide appropriate remedial help. Parents can be of enormous assistance by providing extra practice in the areas concerned (in co-operation with the school, and taking care not to stress the child), and by assuring the child of their unqualified belief in him or her as a person. Children with learning difficulties all too often suffer from low self-confidence, and, like gifted children, can become isolated and depressed. Provided that they are assured at all times that they have the love and belief of their parents (and of their siblings if any), the risks of these things happening are greatly reduced.

Sometimes children with learning difficulties become very frustrated with everything to do with learning, and may develop behaviour problems as a way of compensating for their lack of progress. The rules for dealing with the situation are the same as for all good parenting. The child concerned needs understanding and patience, and at the same time the application of consistent, fair, and where necessary firm standards. He or she must not be allowed to use learning difficulties as an excuse for bad behaviour, but at the same time must be assured that adults understand the particular challenges to which these difficulties give rise. Children should never be expected to have the emotional maturity and understanding of adults. Life can be hugely daunting for them at times. But problems only become insuperable if the child is left to feel that others fail to understand the nature and impact of these problems.

A vital need for all children, whatever their abilities, is an acceptable level of self-esteem (Chapter 3). Children must be able to think well of themselves. When working with either troubled adults or children, the problem in almost all cases comes back to (or closely involves) an inability genuinely to value the self. In the absence of self-esteem we have self-rejection and even self-disgust. Children who show the most extreme behaviour problems (including delinquent behaviours) characteristically have very low self-esteem. Their 'tough' behaviour is often a form of self-defence, while their bitterness towards society and its values is a reflection of their bitterness towards themselves. This is not a way of excusing such behaviours, but a way of explaining their presence and a pointer towards their avoidance, namely a realization that all children need the experience of success, and need to learn through success rather than through failure. Children with learning difficulties have a particular need for this success, and only in its absence are real problems likely to develop.

The golden rule when teaching children with learning difficulties (it applies to parents just as much as to teachers) is therefore that such children must be enabled to experience success *at however low an initial level*. With this experience of success comes an increase in self-belief, an increase of interest in learning, and an increase in enthusiasm for life generally. Once success has become established, standards can be allowed gently to rise, so that the child (at an appropriate pace) is enabled progressively to aim higher. Even the most gifted of us uses only a fraction of our full mental potential. No matter how slow-learning children may be, they always have unused potential. They can always perform above their present level – very often spectacularly so – provided they are given the right learning opportunities. It is sometimes said with reason that there are no bad learners, only bad teachers. If a child fails to learn, it is because we as adults have failed to present material in a form suited to his or her present abilities, and have failed to go at a pace suited to his or her levels of understanding.

CHAPTER 7

The Child and God

THE NATURAL RELIGION OF CHILDHOOD

The great endeavours of the human mind spring from natural forces that are present with us at birth. As we saw in the last two chapters this is so of science and of the arts, and so it is of religion. Children are naturally religious. Their recognition of the mystery and the wonder of life, their contact with the intense, immaterial world of their own thoughts and feelings and dreams, the strength of their motivation to know, their assumption that other forms of consciousness exist besides that of ourselves, their trust in the ability of those stronger than themselves to love and care for them, combine to give a ready acceptance of the existence of God. And to young children, God (or the gods) is not merely an abstract name given to the forces of creation, but a living reality, as much responsible for their presence in the world as are their own fathers and mothers.

As the religious sense is innate within us, children do not learn their concepts of 'god' only from what adults tell them. The concept of a god or gods exists in one form or another in almost all cultures. The problem is, of course, that from their lofty pedestal of rationality, many adults dismiss a child's god-consciousness as simply immature imagination, to be replaced as quickly as possible with the hard reality of adult thinking. Such imagination is seen as akin to the superstitions of primitive peoples, and as a misleading nonsense if allowed to persist into later years.

The assumptions behind this kind of adult thinking are firstly that so-called primitive people, with their 'superstitions', are necessarily more ignorant than we are about spiritual matters.

And secondly that 'imagination' is simply a form of mental wool-gathering, which has nothing to say about the nature of reality. The first of these assumptions, for those who have worked with or studied the spiritual beliefs and practices of early or of non-Western cultures, is manifestly false. And the second, for those who have studied the workings of imagination, is equally untrue.

Imagination is, in fact, one of the most valuable and powerful of all the qualities possessed by the human mind (see Chapter 8). Imagination underlies creativity not just in the arts but also in the sciences, where it demonstrates its ability to spawn new ideas and new inventions. The great scientist produces his or her discoveries not through painstaking experiment, with one thing leading step-by-step to another, but through an intuitive leap of the mind that produces an exciting new theory capable of being put to subsequent experimental test. There is a reason why some scientists speak of the laboratory of the mind, for it is in this laboratory that most of the great advances in human endeavour have their birth.

IMAGINATION AND SPIRITUALITY

Imagination is also now recognized as having similar power in the field of human psychology. In many psychological therapies, a vital step is often to help the client to *imagine* him- or herself as successfully overcoming whatever psychological problems or challenges lie in their path. The inner act of imagination, in some way that at present we imperfectly understand, seems capable of programming the mind to overcome difficulties in the outer world. The change in outward action is thus directly initiated by the inner action of imagination. In addition, the psychologist's use of hypnosis relies for its success almost entirely upon awakening the client's powers of imagination. The better the powers of imagination, the more effective the hypnosis.

Similarly, in physical medicine, the act of imagining oneself as well or as fighting off an invading presence in the body can significantly speed actual recovery. And in sport, to imagine oneself as succeeding, as hitting the perfect shot in golf or in tennis, as jumping the intended height, as outwitting the opponent, is now recognized by leading sportsmen and women to be a potent agent in actual achievement.

Thus imagination is far more than mere make-believe. It is a potent creative force that can operate to change lives. And it is imagination that helps keep us in communication with that unseen reality that we call the spiritual. Through imagination children 'know' God in the same way that they 'know' of their own existence. Imagination helps the child to personalize God, and express him or her in human form. God becomes the idealized loving and protecting father or mother. And since a father or a mother has to live somewhere, the child accepts the notion that this somewhere is heaven, a word synonymous in many languages with the sky. So God lives somewhere up above us, from where he or she can look down and see that all is well with us.

This childhood understanding is not as touchingly naive as it may sound. Children do not divide the world into categories in the same way as adults. The sky is indeed up above us, but when a child lies in the long grass of summer and gazes into its blue depths, the sky is not something separate and beyond, but as much a part of personal experience as is the breathing or the beating of the heart. Young children sometimes talk of reaching up to touch the sky. It can seem as near and as intimate to them as the ground under their feet.

EVOLVING IDEAS ABOUT GOD

As children grow older, however, so this idea of a God suspended somewhere up in the blue comes increasingly under attack. They learn of the law of gravity, they learn that a person cannot be in all places at once, or simultaneously see everything that is going on in the world. There cannot, therefore, be a kindly person up in the sky after all. At this point – and it is arrived at in adolescence if not before – the child begins to question the idea of God, and often rejects it in favour of a belief only in an outer reality that can be seen and touched, and that obeys the known laws of science.

The need at this point is for an evolving, developing concept of God, that moves on a stage further in understanding how to express an inner reality in an outward form. Vedanta, one of the oldest and most noble forms of thought practised in Hinduism, teaches that God can be thought of at three levels. In the first, there is God with form and attributes. This is the God who may be imagined as a father or as a mother, or who is fully expressed on earth through the avatar, that is through an incarnation of godliness such as Rama or Krishna or the Buddha or Christ. Then there is God without form but with attributes, who may be thought of in the abstract as perfect love, perfect consciousness, perfect bliss, perfect omnipotence. Finally there is God without form and without attributes, the immortal eternal reality that lies so far beyond the limited power of thought and of language that anything we can say about him/her/it must necessarily be incomplete. The 'God' in fact about whom ultimately nothing can be said, but who can be experienced in the mystical stillness of one's own inner being. The Christian mystics refer to this third level as the Godhead, the Hebrew mystics as Ain Soph, and the Buddhists as the Sambhogakaya.

None of these three levels is necessarily 'superior' to the others, since an absolute God encompasses all three. Each is suitable for a particular stage in the development of our understanding, and each can be used as the focus of our spiritual beliefs and spiritual practices. Even for the same person it is suitable to think of God at different times at each of these three levels, dependent upon the particular needs of the moment. Sometimes we require the comfort and the objective reassurance of God with form, the God who can be presented in religious art and who was personified in the incarnation or incarnations sacred to our particular religion. At other times we need to think of the abstract God, and identify within ourselves the potential for the perfect qualities that he or she represents. At other times still, we need that deep numinous sense of a reality that transcends names and descriptions and yet gives meaning to all other realities, that exists sublime and complete in itself, yet embraces and encompasses all things and extends into an unknown infinity above and beyond rational comprehension.

If it proves difficult to understand how these three levels can all be valid, it is useful to draw an analogy (limited but useful as far as it goes) with the human trinity of body, mind and soul, with body analagous to God with form, mind to God without form but with attributes, and soul to God without form or attributes. Body, mind and soul are each an expression of our personal reality, and to each of them we give attention in a different way and at different times. For the child, there is no need to reject the idea of God as father or mother when the time comes to move on to the concept of God without form but with attributes. The image of the ideal father or mother is still an appropriate way of symbolizing God. And when (and if – since many people do not aspire to this third level) the child moves to the realization of God without form and without attributes, it is not necessary to reject the idea of God with attributes. Our own understanding of the nature of such divine attributes as love and compassion help shape our ideals and guide our conduct towards our fellow men and women.

TALKING TO CHILDREN ABOUT GOD

When we talk about God to children, or answer their questions, we should keep in mind their level of understanding. The above three ways of conceptualizing God express these levels, and thus serve as our essential guide. But they are also vital to our own sense of the spiritual. Many adults lost their religious faith when, as children, they decided that the idea of an old man or woman up in the sky was untenable, but unfortunately had nothing to put in its place. The fault lies largely in our culture, which has turned its back on the true meaning and use of symbolism. God as father or as mother is a symbol, and the value of a powerful symbol of this kind is that although it stands for a reality beyond itself, it provides us with a key that helps us approach nearer to that reality. It is not an arbitrary invention of the mind, in the way of a company logo or trademark, but a manifestation of the language of the unconscious mind.

Thus 'father' or 'mother' occur spontaneously as symbols for God in many cultures. And the more we meditate on the qualities of an ideal parent, the more these symbols provide us with an intuitive understanding (and worship) of godliness – and also help us to look more closely at our own behaviour as parents. This is not a recipe for making ourselves feel inadequate. To recognize and admit to our imperfections is a sign of strength and not of weakness, and allows us to start working sensibly and realistically on these imperfections. We are not saints, but to have an understanding of the spiritual ideal of parenthood gives us a measure against which to set our own behaviour, and a goal towards which to aspire.

Some parents are afraid that if they use the symbolism of God as father or as mother they risk saddling God in the child's mind with their own shortcomings. But here again the child's imagination is a useful quality, because it allows him or her to picture someone with all the positive attributes of parents but without the negative, and also helps them the better to honour their parents, since parenthood is the chosen symbol of divinity and of the creative power of divinity.

Other spiritual symbols besides that of God as father or mother are also of great value to the child. The cross, holy pictures, rupas, all help the child to think about God, just as a name helps us to think about a friend. From an early age, children can be encouraged to draw and paint these symbols. Research into the spontaneous scribblings of young children indicates that the cross and the circle, both of which have almost universally been used as symbols of divinity, occur naturally from an early age. There is something satisfying to children about these signs even before they understand their religious significance. In fact it is better not to discuss this significance too soon. The symbols are best left to speak for themselves through their direct relationship with the child's unconscious.

Children can also be encouraged to gather symbols from nature. There is something satisfying to a child in smooth round stones for example, in feathers and in pine cones, and in skeletonized leaves and curiously shaped pieces of wood. At Christmas the holly and mistletoe and fir trees that are brought into the house are also sources of interest and pleasure, and serve as natural reminders of the mystic nature of this special time of year. Children can be encouraged to see in them and in the growth, flowering and seeding of plants and trees during the other seasons the outward symbol of the life-force.

Young children have little difficulty with the notion of symbolism (Chapter 2). Symbolism is for them a natural extension of the 'let's pretend' world of childhood in which one thing, through the power of the imagination, readily stands for another. In earlier generations this was even more apparent than it is today, for to children without toys a favourite piece of wood served very well as a doll, a boat, a gun, a castle, in fact as virtually anything desired by a young and fertile imagination.

All the great symbols disclose many different levels of meaning for those who care to look for them. Symbolically, to the small child God is the heavenly father or mother, but even a very young child can understand that this is only one way of thinking of Him or Her. Children will readily accept that God is also the force that makes the flowers grow, the birds sing, the sun shine, the rain fall, and winter turn into spring. They will accept that God gives the love that we feel for each other, the good that we do, the kindness, grace and compassion of the human family. This early experience of a form of pantheism (God in all things) prepares children for the more abstract, mystical levels of understanding that come later.

THE USE OF ANALOGY

Children also readily accept that, just as we can talk *about* God, so we can talk *to* God. No child has difficulty with the idea of talking to someone who is not physically present. Many children have imaginary playmates, and to all children the characters in stories and in rhymes continue to exist outside the pages that brought them to life. To young children, prayer is like talking to a wise, all-seeing adult, and the act of regular prayer helps them to feel more deeply the reality of the spiritual life.

As God is a real presence to children, before long they begin to ask such questions as 'How can God be everywhere all at the same time?' 'Does God know everything we do?' 'Who made God?' 'Does God grow old?' and so on. As in all answers to children's questions, honesty is the golden rule. If we know the answer, we should give it, and put it in language that the child can understand. And we should remember always the power of these answers. Small children are highly impressionable, and what we say to them now may influence their thinking for many years to come (how often do we catch ourselves trotting out an answer that we heard long ago in primary school, and which we have never re-examined in the light of more mature understanding).

It is also good to give children analogies from something they already know. Analogy is one of the most useful ways of answering all childhood questions, no matter what the subject and no matter what the level of enquiry. So God can be in more than one place just as the wind can be in more than one place, and water can be in more than one place, and the sky can be in more than one place. Unlike adults, children tend not to pursue questions beyond the point at which they have received useful information, but should the child then go on to ask if God is like the wind and like the water and like the sky, the answer is yes, and also like everything else in creation. A child finds it much easier to accept that everything is a part of God than to imagine that God made the world out of some kind of 'stuff' that was separate from Him/Her. The idea of such 'stuff' not only prompts questions a little later on as to where this 'stuff' came from if it was not part of God in the first place but also doubts as to how God can be infinite and all-powerful if the world and we ourselves are made of something separate from Him/Her, and that just happened to be conveniently lying around at the time of creation.

However, there are many questions about God that we may feel unable to answer, and if so we should say so. It is misleading to give children the impression in any area of life that we know everything, and only courts disillusion in the years to come, when they inevitably discover that we are after all only fallible human beings. So in response to those questions we can't answer it is best to say 'I don't know, and I wonder about that myself'; or 'I *think* the answer is . . . but I'm just not sure', or 'I really don't know; there are lots of mysteries about God and about the world; perhaps one day you'll be the one who finds out some of the answers for us.'

THE PROBLEM OF EVIL

Sooner or later, the children will wonder how, if God is love, He/She allows bad things to happen in the world. The old answer was that there are two forces at work in creation, the good and the bad, and that there is a constant war between them, with God and the angels on one side, and Satan and his army on the other. If we side with God we one day go to our reward in heaven, and if we side with Satan we are condemned to eternal torments in hell. Irrespective for a moment of the rights and wrongs of this argument, there is no doubt that it was used as a potent force of social control, not only by the church with its people, but by adults with children. If you were good (meaning usually obedient), you stored up merit in heaven, but if you were bad (usually disobedient), you received black marks in God's book, and one day were taken off to the fires of damnation.

Many a child grew up filled with guilt and terror as a result of such teachings, and the idea of a merciful God of love somehow became lost behind that of a vengeful God who created people only one day to see them suffer everlasting torture. Newer (and – if we go back in time – much older) teachings tell us that the flames of hell are a symbol for the remorse we feel when one day we recognize the suffering we have caused to others, or the opportunities we have missed for bringing them comfort and happiness. Hell is a state of mind rather than a state of body, and far from being eternal it is part of the (often painful) learning that we have all to undertake on our long journey of spiritual growth.

This does not, however, immediately dispose of the problem of evil, since a child as he or she grows older is prone to ask why does the world have to be made that way? Why couldn't God make it perfect from the start? The argument that we will only be able to appreciate perfection when we have first known imperfection is unsatisfying, since it only leads to the question why should this be so? If perfection is perfection, then it should not need to depend upon the prior existence of imperfection. If it does, how can it be perfection?

One reply that we increasingly hear these days, particularly from New Age teachers, is that everything is already perfect, and that we only need a mystical insight into reality to understand it. This is a variant of the old teaching that everything is God's 'will' and must be accepted as such, and is unlikely to be greeted with much favour by the socially concerned adolescent, who will immediately demand to know how this fits in with the famine, violence and misery suffered by many millions of people in underprivileged and war-torn parts of the world.

The most practical answer to the problem of evil is much less high-flown. It is simply that we have the power of free-will, and that free-will, at least in the limited way in which we understand it, expresses itself through choice. In life we are each confronted with a series of choices, and it is up to us to make these choices in a wise and socially useful way. Instead of asking unanswerable questions as to why suffering, whatever its causes, should be allowed to exist in the world, the question should always be 'What can I choose to do in order to make the world a better place?'

As we saw in Chapter 4, the power of the personal choices we make in life, and the nature of the results that stem from them, can often best be brought home to a child through what is called the law of natural consequences. If a toy is wilfully or carelessly broken, the owner has (for a time at least) to live without it. If a child is too busy playing or watching television to come to the table and eat the food that has been prepared, hunger will be experienced until the next meal time comes round. Natural consequences, when used sensibly and when the child is no physical danger, teach humanely and realistically that we must think carefully about the choices we make in life, and bear some responsibility for their outcomes.

Of course, children soon become aware that some people appear able to indulge in all kinds of bad behaviour and get away with it, and this enrages their ideas of fair-play. But the appropriate reply to this is that the child is responsible for his or her own behaviour, and is not called upon to answer for the thoughtless or unsocial actions of others. The natural consequence may catch up with the wrong-doers in later years, or, if we believe in wider and richer horizons than the cradle and the grave, in a life to come. It is fruitless to worry about errors made by others and outside our control. 'Do what *you* can to help the world', is always the best advice to the child, 'however great or small'. Influence others for good certainly, give them all the help you can, but don't feel cheated simply because they seem to escape the consequences of breaking those rules of unselfish conduct that you try always to obey.

It is also appropriate to remind children that they have no knowledge of the inner lives of others, or of the difficulties that others may have had – and may have – to face in life. No one can know precisely how much freedom of choice another person has got, or whether they have had as much help in making properly informed decisions as we have ourselves.

SELF-ASSERTION AND SELFLESSNESS

Of course, as parents we suffer through our children, and when we see others gaining unfair advantage over them, or exploiting them in some way, we feel natural outrage. We have no wish to turn our children into docile little creatures who can't stand up for themselves against the injustices of the world. There must always be a proper balance between the rights of others and the rights of oneself. If children are always expected, for example, to give way before the demands made by peers and by adults, then in no sense can they be said to retain their freedom of choice. So there must be a balance between self-assertion on the one hand and selflessness on the other. Self-assertion is the ability to defend one's legitimate rights, and selflessness is the ability to place the needs of others before our own. Both qualities depend in large degree upon the successful completion of the tasks of childhood described in Chapters 3 and 4, but they also depend upon the learned ability to discriminate between what is legitimate social behaviour and what is not.

However, self-assertion should always involve the assertion of a self that is worth asserting. And such a self will always carry within it a recognition of the value of compassion, sympathy and understanding towards others. It cannot be true to itself if it forces its own concerns needlessly upon others, puts itself always first on principle, and is deaf to the needs of other people when these needs prove inconvenient. A self that is conscious of its shared humanity with the rest of creation finds that a balance between self-assertion and selflessness comes, if not always easily, at least always with clarity and conviction.

Children should not have more demanded of them in this respect than they are capable of giving, but children have a natural sense of the needs of others. Watch the distress of a small child seeing a friend in tears or an animal in pain. Notice how in such circumstances most children will run to help, or to summon an adult. We start physical life quite literally as a part of two other people, and although we grow into individuality this sense of being joined to others, and through them to the rest of the human race, remains deeply embedded within us. We are thus compassionate and empathic towards others by nature. But we are also imbued with the will to fight for our personal survival, and it is in obtaining and keeping a balance between these two instinctive forces that we become properly human, and learn how to contribute fully towards the betterment of the human race.

One of the best ways of teaching this balance is through example. Much of a child's most valuable learning comes through watching and copying what others do, and the more he or she loves and respects the people concerned, the more likely he or she is to follow their lead. If adults demonstrate to children in practical ways the extent of their concern for the welfare of family, neighbours, friends and all those in need, the natural sensitivity of children develops accordingly. Above all of course, it is essential we show towards children the qualities we want them to show towards others. Much bad education in schools is the result of teachers who extol the virtues of kindness and justice only to show no signs of either when relating to the children in their care. Just as children best learn to love by being loved, so they best learn all other desirable qualities by personally experiencing their value.

Another essential aid to helping young children learn the balance between self and others is once again the use of stories and pictures. Not 'improving' stories with unbelievable characters, but stories containing heroes and heroines with whom children can identify. Like watching and copying the behaviour of parents, children enjoy imitating that of the fictional characters they admire, whether these be portrayed as people or as animals. By imaginatively putting themselves into the roles concerned, they absorb both consciously and unconsciously many of the attitudes and values involved.

Children also enjoy discussing the rights and wrongs of particular actions. One of the best ways of starting these discussions is with 'what if?' stories. 'What if some older children frightened a boy into giving them his pocket money, and threatened to beat him up if he told anyone; what should he do?' 'What if a girl had a best friend, and they shared their secrets with each other, and the friend went and told the girl's secrets to other people; should the girl give away her friend's secrets to get her own back?' 'What if a girl had some money for her lunch on a school outing, and a girl she didn't know very well had forgotten her money and asked her to share; what should she do?' 'What if a boy found a toy that he liked very much and wanted to keep, but he knew the owner was very upset at having lost it; should he own up and give the toy back?' 'What if a girl had a best friend, but the best friend always insisted they do the things she wanted to do; how should the girl react?'

These and similar stories present clearly the conflict between self-assertion and selflessness, and although the answers to them seem obvious enough to us, to young children such stories provide material for endless discussion and debate, and the answers they give will vary with their ages and with their levels of understanding. Before the age or seven or eight, it is less important that they give the 'right' answers than that they are helped to think deeply about the issues concerned. What should a child do if confronted by the situations in the stories? Should he or she put self first or not? What are the real issues involved? What part would (or should) friendship or fear or any other feelings play in their decisions? What would be the likely outcomes of these decisions? And so on.

Much of life involves conflicts between our own interests and the interests of others, and a large part not only of our social responsibility but also of our intimate relationships and of our self-respect is determined by the way in which we resolve them. Initially such resolution comes from the thought and the debate that goes into answering questions of the kind just presented, but in adolescence children become conscious that the conflict also requires us to see each social action (perhaps indeed each human action) as affecting not just ourselves and those close to us, but also a wide range of our fellow human beings. Like a stone setting up ripples in a pond, each action has repercussions far outside the sphere of our own self-interest. Once we see humanity not as a collection of separate individuals but as a far-reaching unity, much as a piece of music is a unity rather than a collection of individual notes, then the larger part of the self–other dilemma disappears, to be replaced by a clearer understanding and acceptance of what is and is not appropriate in each social situation.

GRATITUDE

Crucial to a realization of this unity is the experience of gratitude towards other people for all the things they do for us. Gratitude implies an effective recognition of these things, and a sincere feeling of thanks in response. Many parents complain of the ingratitude their children show, but often this ingratitude is less wilfulness on the child's part than a genuine failure to appreciate the emotional and physical costs of parenthood. Young children have only their own limited experience upon which to draw, and this does not of course include parenthood! Unaware fully of what it means to be a parent, children tend to take much of what a parent does for them for granted, and to become increasingly confused and resentful in the face of constant reminders of all the gratitude they are supposed to be feeling.

However, children are not by nature ungrateful, and whether they learn to express this gratitude or not depends in part upon how we show our gratitude for having them. For we also can take things for granted. Men and women have natural parental instincts, and few parents can remain unmoved by the sufferings of those who try unsuccessfully to conceive, or who have actually lost a child through accident or illness. The death of a child can bring perhaps the deepest levels of grief and suffering known to mankind, and even when most at odds with their children the recognition of this is enough to set most parents counting their blessings.

Gratitude is a wonderful emotion in that it renders good actions natural and spontaneous. To feel gratitude for our children is one of the best ways of helping ourselves to remain patient with them, to want to spend time with them, to share and encourage their interests, and – perhaps above all – to teach them that gratitude can be a two-way process. Even the most secure children need reassurance that their presence in the world is welcome, and that we are glad to have them around, and value their ideas, their help, their conversation, their ability to raise our spirits, their fresh and exciting way of looking at the world, their good humour, their love and affection. By showing ourselves grateful for these things, we allow our children to feel wanted and valued, to recognize that they have important things to offer to life, and that the world is a better place because of them.

We can also help children by showing our gratitude for life's other gifts. It is unfortunately true that we tend only to value something fully when we have lost it. Many of the things we take each day for granted would be prized beyond words by large numbers of our fellow men and women. In the morning we have the health and strength to get out of bed and stand on our own two feet. We open our eyes and see the world. We listen to the sounds of the world. We run up and down the stairs, we feed and toilet ourselves, we enjoy our food, we bend down to tie our shoe laces, we use our hands and our fingers to pick up and to manipulate things, we make use of the gift of speech. How many people less fortunate than ourselves would love to be able to do these simple, everyday, infinitely precious things!

Such things allow us to enjoy life and its beauties. The wide sweep of the sky, the shape of clouds, the green leaves of spring and the reds and golds of autumn. The sight and scent of flowers in summer. The wind from the south and the rain on the window. The pleasures of walking on the uplands, or following a path through the woods. The glow of city lights on a winter evening. The waves breaking on a rocky shore, and the moon over a silver sea. All these things should move the spirit into a prayer of thanksgiving.

And so should the love of family and friends, the joy of music and of poetry, the beauties of art and of sculpture, the magnificence of cathedrals and great architecture, the pleasures of sport and human achievement, the courage and vision and self-sacrifice of others, the benefits of science and medicine. These things are so much a part of life that we rarely stop to think how barren existence would be without them. Yet stop and think we must, if we are to value them as we should.

Expressions of gratitude by adults draw children's attention to the benefits they enjoy themselves. Once we are aware of gratitude it finds spontaneous expression, whether in the form of words, of reverence, of song and poetry, or of service to others. It is not difficult for a young child to identify with this expression. Young children feel a natural delight in being alive. It is visible in the way they move, in the pleasure they show on receiving a special treat, in their play, in their enjoyment of friends. The intense urge of a child to participate in life is a direct result of this delight, and a direct affirmation of the human spirit.

Many parents like children to express gratitude through prayer, and this is invaluable provided the thanks comes directly from the child. Prayers can become mechanical and meaningless if they consist only of the repetition of a list of 'thank-yous' to God for a whole range of things catalogued for the child by a presiding adult. Far better to help children think back over the day, and say words of their own choosing for the things especially enjoyed. Parents can then add their own reasons for thanks. Prayer need never be formal, particularly in the company of children. A young mind can identify more readily with prayers that speak to God as if to a sympathetic friend rather than to a remote authoritarian figure waiting to pounce upon every omission. The act of prayer works an inner magic in the heart, and it is best thought of in this way rather than as a tribute demanded by God. Prayer gives extra strength to our lives, and helps us remember that it is the fact of life itself for which we should feel most thankfulness.

THE CONCEPT OF ETERNAL LIFE

Closely linked to all the great spiritual traditions of the world is the concept that life, in one form or another, goes on after the death of the physical body. Children have a ready acceptance of the idea of immortality, whether it is mentioned to them in connection with the death of a close relative at one end of the scale or that of a small household pet at the other. Some psychologists suggest this is because a child cannot imagine the idea of his or her own non-existence, but as a child experiences dream-less sleep for part of every night, this seems rather unconvincing. A more likely explanation is that, being alive, we all have an intuitive understanding of what life really *is*. And this intuitive understanding gives us the assurance – unless and until we are conditioned to believe otherwise – that life is more than simply the material body.

I often stress to parents that although they themselves may have lost their belief in an after-life, it is unfair to impose this belief upon children. Far better for children to stay with their own intuitive understanding until such time as they are able to question and assess it for themselves. At the very least, no one can prove there is no life after death, while on the other hand the teachings of the great spiritual leaders and mystics, together with the evidence built up over the centuries by post-mortem communications (many of them highly veridical), point very strongly in the other direction.

The acceptance by children of a life after death leads them in due course to wonder what this life will be like. Most traditions suggest it involves some kind of judgement, in which our behaviour in our present lives helps determine what is to come. Children, however, should never be frightened into believing stories of eternal damnation. Adults still tell me of the horrors they experienced as children on hearing these stories, and of the attempts made by adults to shock them into being 'good' by accounts, medieval in concept and in detail, of hell fire and damnation.

More enlightened modern teachings suggest that the torments

of which our ancestors spoke are symbolic, and consist of the mental anguish experienced when we fully understand the consequences for others of our thoughtless or unfeeling actions. Buddhism and other Eastern traditions have always taught that in any case the suffering caused by this anguish is not permanent, and that having experienced full remorse, the individual is then free to progress to the next stage in his or her spiritual journey.

In the Christian gospels references to hell fire are restricted to St Matthew (who incidentally refers to the fire as being 'eternal', and not the punishment of the sinner), and in the Revised Version the word 'hell' is replaced in places by 'Hades', the barren and forsaken underworld of the Greeks, a place of penance and sadness. In the Old Testament the word used is 'shaoul', the lost, shadowy underworld of the Hebrews. Christ himself says specifically that 'no sin, no slander is beyond the forgiveness for men' except for 'whoever slanders the Holy Spirit . . . he is guilty of eternal sin' (*New English Bible*), which makes perfect sense, since 'slandering the Holy Spirit' stands for the total rejection of the spiritual life, and as long as this rejection persists, there can be no opportunity for redemption. Yet note that even here it is the sin that is 'eternal' and not the guilt of the sinner. The slander against the Holy Spirit can never be other than a sin; the sinner, however, can give up the sin, and in so doing accept the reality of the spiritual life, and find his or her way back to spiritual growth.

We should thus never frighten children (or ourselves) with the threat of eternal damnation, or with threats of a vengeful God who creates human beings in order to condemn many of them to an eternity of suffering. Christ speaks of God as 'love', and even our imperfect human understanding of love cannot encompass a God who would treat creation in this way. True goodness arises out of the love that enables us, like the great spiritual teachers down the ages, to show infinite compassion towards others, to understand that they share the same humanity as ourselves, and to put their well-being beyond that of ourselves. The great traditions all speak of the need to 'die to self', that is to find the true spirituality within ourselves that transcends the selfish needs of the personal ego, and knows the ultimate unity of all being.

If 'hell' is thus a state of mind (which can be experienced in this life and not only in the life to come), the same is true of heaven. Many children as they grow older find it hard to conceive of a heaven that consists solely of people praising God. Questions arise as to what else people *do* there, and whether in the end we are likely to become bored if there are no challenges and no new opportunities. Experiences in deep levels of meditation (discussed more fully in due course) indicate that the mind can reach a level beyond thought, and experience indescribable states of bliss in which everything becomes elevated into an awareness of pure love that permeates all things and at the same time lies outside space and time. Mystics from both East and West have written of this state, and it probably provides the best descriptions that we have of the Kingdom of Heaven. Not a 'place' where we are subject to the concepts and feelings of the physical world, but an experience beyond all experiences.

Those 'communications' from the next world that suggest it is rather like the present one would seem to be from individuals whose minds are still full of the concepts of material existence. Their thoughts literally create their other-world reality, and their accounts of their experiences indicate that much learning and spiritual journeying lie ahead of them. Eastern religions (with the exception of Islam) teach that part of this journeying consists of a return to this world (reincarnation), since this is the only place where struggles and challenges face us, and therefore the only place where certain kinds of learning are possible. Whether one accepts these teachings or not is very much a matter of personal choice, but at the very least they carry the symbolic message that learning and development do not cease with physical death, and that there is no final judgement on the basis of the experiences of one earthly life. They also incidentally carry the message that judgement is in a sense a personal undertaking, built into the logic of the system, rather than something handed down by a sort of glorified court of law. In Christ's words: 'As you sow, so you shall reap'.

As with their ideas of God, children's ideas of heaven should be allowed to develop as they grow older. Initially they will tend to think of it as a beautiful city or garden, rather like the paradise conditions sometimes presented in their story books. Later they will perhaps see it as a place of spiritual progress, rather like a distant country to be travelled and explored. Later still they may come to think of it as an experience beyond the limited concepts of the human mind, something that can only be known by being known. But whatever their concepts, the most important thing is that children preserve their sense of themselves as immortal beings. Nothing has the power to influence our view of ourselves and of existence like the concept of a destiny that transcends the limited experiences of the present life. Without this concept, life is quite literally bounded by the cradle and the grave, and its purpose and meaning limited by the same parameters. The most sublime teachings given by men and women, the highest achievements in art, the most noble and selfless actions, have stemmed from those whose thoughts were not bounded in this way. Their beliefs and their certainties have enriched our present lives, and helped us prepare for what lies beyond, and ultimately it is for each person to form his or her own judgement as to whether their legacy to us is to be accepted or not.

CHAPTER 8

Magic, Terrors and Dreaming

THE MEDIEVAL WORLD OF THE CHILD

Young children live in a world not unlike that inhabited by adults in medieval times. They have no rights to their own property, no say in how to spend the hours from nine to four, and no guaranteed financial return for their labours. They are unenfranchised, subject to arbitrary and often unfair punishments (including legalized physical violence), face lawlessness from peers (with potential danger lurking around each corner), and suffer greatly from the indifference, disapproval or disdain of the ruling (adult) classes. In addition, they see the world in the pre-scientific way in which medieval people saw it, with no clear boundaries between imagination and reality, and no firm distinction between human consciousness and the rest of creation (see Chapter 2).

But the medieval world did have its compensations. In medieval times there was a colour and a poetry to life, an excitement and – for all its squalor – a grandeur that is missing from our more organized and more predictable world. We find it in writers of the time such as Chaucer and Boccaccio, and Shakespeare captures it in the historical plays. There was also a mystery. For with their pre-scientific view of the world, medieval men and women accepted largely without question the existence of unseen forces (both good and evil), and their own immortality.

Experiments carried out some years ago by Gertrude Schmeidler in the USA (and repeated at various times by other researchers) suggest that a belief in the existence of these unseen powers (we refer to them nowadays by the terms telepathy, clairvoyance and precognition) may help us to experience them, and it may be the very fact of their faith in an unseen world that helped people in medieval times to feel its reality. If we continue the parallel with childhood, it may be that the essentially medieval world-view of young children allows them to use abilities that fade in later years as rationality closes the mind to the possibility of their existence.

Parents sometimes comment not only on the apparent knowing nature of very young children but also on the fact that they claim to see playmates invisible to the rest of us, or strange nocturnal visitors, or apparitions of recently deceased relatives or pets. Usually such claims are dismissed as no more than childish fantasy, and the child's insistences met with disbelief or active disapproval. Such things do not exist, therefore the child must be imagining or deliberately inventing them.

PSYCHIC ABILITIES

Yet the reality of certain kinds of psychic ability (extrasensory perception – or ESP for short) is now accepted by many reputable scientists as established beyond reasonable doubt, and established moreover on the basis of research evidence collected under the most stringently controlled conditions. Adults who possess psychic gifts often claim that these gifts were present in childhood, and that until they learned otherwise they assumed everyone possessed them. So how seriously should we take children's claims to be able to see things we can't see, or know things we don't know?

There is no doubt that children can confuse fiction with fact. And there is no doubt that they sometimes invent imaginary playmates to compensate for loneliness, or to give them a friend they can control as they please, or simply as an excuse for their own behaviour (it was the friend who committed the misdemeanour, or who suggested it to them). But this does not give us grounds for dismissing everything as fantasy. Ian Stevenson, of the University of Virginia, has spent many years following up the cases of children who, as early in some cases as the third year of life, spontaneously begin to talk of a previous life, and who give details (such as name, location, and the identity of relatives) that can be verified by careful research. With young children one can be reasonably sure that these details are not the result of normally acquired information, and Stevenson has been able to show that in a large number of cases they check out well with the facts.

Sometimes the children even have physical attributes (such as birth marks or disabilities or the susceptibility to certain infections) that appear to relate to the manner in which they 'died' in their previous lives.

Usually these early memories begin to fade by around the sixth or seventh year of life. Whether they support the idea of reincarnation or not is a matter of debate, but they certainly suggest that the children concerned have ESP abilities of one kind or another. Possibly they are able telepathically to gather information from the memories of relatives and friends of the deceased (though why they should unconsciously and unintentionally then translate these memories into a previous life of their own is not clear), or even to contact the memories of the deceased person in the afterlife. In the East (many of Stevenson's cases come from India), and in the Western mystery traditions, there is a belief in what are called the Akashic Records, allegedly an account of everything that has ever happened on earth, and should such records exist in some form as yet unknown to science it is possible that the child gleans information from them. But for present purposes the *how* of the child's information is not particularly relevant. What is far more important is its very existence. Some children do appear to have what are generally called psychic gifts, gifts that usually disappear by around age six.

What should a parent do if a child claims to see or to talk to invisible presences, or to give any other signs of ESP? Should the child be praised, discouraged, or simply ignored? The answer depends in part upon the parent's own attitude towards psychic gifts. Some of the scientists who accept their existence regard them as vestigial traces of an ability possessed by primitive humankind but long since rendered redundant by the development of speech, written language and other forms of more sophisticated accurate communication. In their view, little good is served by taking notice of anything so fleeting and erratic, and that in consequence appears to tell us little about the workings of the human mind. Other scientists, however, consider psychic abilities are potentially of great importance, since they stand outside the known laws of science and pose a major challenge to our understanding of reality. Yet other scientists go further, and suggest that since they do not appear to use physical channels, they support the idea that mind is non-material and may therefore transcend the life and death of the brain and the body.

In view of the implications of this last suggestion, the neglect of ESP by organized Western religions comes as a surprise. Attitudes range from indifference on the one hand (what has ESP got to do with spirituality?) to outright hostility on the other (such powers must be from Satan). For the parent, however, the emphasis should be upon the needs of the child. Even if you flatly disbelieve in any form of ESP, children who claim to see invisible playmates, or dead relatives or neighbours, must be listened to with the same attention and interest that are given to accounts of their other experiences. If the child speaks about them seriously, it is obvious that to him or her they are real enough. The child should then be questioned about them, in just the way that a child is questioned about other experiences. If the subject is a deceased person known to parents, the child can be asked for details. What was the person wearing? What did they say? How did they look? It was only by questioning children carefully, and taking their replies seriously, that Ian Stevenson was able to establish that many of the details they gave as a result of apparent ESP actually proved to be correct.

In some cases the results will be inconclusive. The child may have seen something objective or not, we can't be sure. But provided the experiences are not being used as a way of gaining attention or of frightening others, they should be listened to at face value. Failure to do this will, at the very least, prevent a child from confiding similar experiences in future, and may also terrify him or her into believing that there is something dark and sinister inside the self about which no one is prepared to give any help. Either way, the child is likely to fight hard to suppress psychic gifts, and to remember them in later life only as one of the odd aberrations of an over-fertile imagination.

If you are convinced of the existence of ESP, or have an open mind about it, you may wonder if there is anything you should do to develop these abilities your child seems to possess. The answer to that is emphatically no. Listen to your child, question him or her, but avoid giving him or her any indication that these abilities are in any way special. You will find in any case that they will probably surface only rarely (perhaps on no more than one or two occasions throughout the whole of childhood), but however infrequently or frequently they occur, a child has enough learning to do in order to cope effectively with the material world, without trying to develop gifts that we imperfectly understand and that could have a distracting effect upon him or her. If children ask questions about these gifts, it is sufficient to say that some people have them, but we aren't sure how they work. Encourage children to let you know if they have ESP experiences, but don't suggest they try and seek them out. Later on in life they can decide for themselves whether they want to try and develop them further or not.

GHOSTS, FAIRIES, AND ROBBERS UNDER THE BED

Irrespective of whether they have ESP experiences of their own or not, all children are fascinated by the idea of ghosts and seem to have an inborn fear of the supernatural. This may be nature's way of deterring us from dabbling too freely in the non-material world, or part of a general fear of the unknown. The reaction of many adults is to tell the child that ghosts don't exist, so there is nothing to worry about. But story books, the spine-chilling tales that children share with each other, and perhaps some innate instinct, all tell the child differently. On a dark night, with the wind howling outside and trees tapping against the window, or the stairs creaking in a silent house, all children *know* that there are ghosts, and that ghosts are generally up to no good. Like all childhood fears, this one must be taken seriously. It is real enough to the child, however unfounded we consider it to be, and the child needs help in coping with it.

This help is best provided by adults who are prepared always to listen to the child, to walk carefully around the house with him or her, looking into every nook and cranny and satisfying everyone that there is nothing and nobody there. When children grow older, they can also be helped to understand that if there are such things as ghosts, there is no reason to believe they mean us any harm. We should credit them with the positive feelings and emotions towards children possessed by the great majority of people in our own world.

There is often an important difference between this fear of ghosts, and the fear of witches, giants, monsters, and robbers hiding under the bed. These last fears often symbolize those aspects of the adult world that the young child is unable to come to terms with at a rational level. Children who have an excessive preoccupation with these aggressive beings are therefore likely to be indicating that they require help in dealing with negative feelings towards grown-ups. These feelings can be the result of parents who switch too swiftly and unpredictably from a benevolent to a punitive role, with too great a contrast between the two, or of parents who are simply too strict and overpowering. Either way, the child feels it hard to reconcile the loving parent with the punitive parent (Chapter 2). To him or her, they are like two separate beings inhabiting the same body.

Whichever the reason, it must be identified and an effort made to be more sensitive to its effect upon the child. Even an excessive fear of the dark may suggest something is leaving the child with feelings of insecurity and threat. Some psychologists suggest that a fear of witches may symbolize a fear of the mother, and a fear of ogres and giants that of the father. The child is thus dealing with a fear of one or other parent by displacing it onto these symbolic figures. Since the child has 'permission' to dislike these figures, feelings of anger towards parents can also be displaced, thus lessening the the child's burden of guilt. However, neither form of displacement allows the child to relate comfortably and honestly to parents, or to develop a more mature and realistic way of dealing with negative feelings and emotions.

A child who is confident at all times of parental love and of the predictability of parental behaviour is unlikely to suffer too deeply from terrors of this kind.

POLTERGEIST DISTURBANCES

An occasional manifestation of psychic activity sometimes blamed on young or adolescent children goes under the term *poltergeist*. The word is German for 'noisy spirit', and refers to those strange unaccountable outbreaks of activity during which objects may be moved, strange rappings and bangings heard, missiles thrown, and even small fires started, without any known human agency being involved. Such phenomena have been reported with great consistency down through the centuries and right across cultures. In medieval times these disturbances were thought to be the work of the devil, outraged by the sanctity of good men and women, as they often seemed to focus upon the households of ministers of religion or other holy people. We now know that many such outbreaks, if at times inconvenient and irritating, are relatively harmless. In fact some victims of poltergeist activity claim to become quite attached to the 'entity' involved, and in some instances there is evidence that 'it' is trying to be helpful, for example, making rudimentary attempts to lay the kitchen table while the occupants of the house are sleeping (the similarities with the so-called 'little people' of Celtic folklore, who were said to help with the cleaning and other household chores if treated with respect, is a fascinating one).

One explanation for poltergeists is that they represent in a way unknown to science the exteriorized emotional energy of the people in whose households they manifest their presence. Adolescents in particular go through a phase of extreme emotional upheaval, with sexual energies and desires – together with the urge for independence and self-expression – at their peak. The argument is that at such a time their feelings of restlessness and frustration can directly affect their environment. Instead of physically throwing the crockery about or tearing up their bed-linen in rage, their mind does the job for them (albeit without their conscious awareness).

In the absence of any more scientific explanation, this one is perhaps as good as any. A more esoteric suggestion is that the poltergeist is an 'earthbound' spirit, someone who has died but is still over-attached to this world and refuses to move on to wherever it is he or she should go. Thus poltergeist activity is attention-seeking behaviour on the part of the spirit concerned, or an expression of outrage that other people should now be living in what the spirit still regards as 'his' or 'her' home. People who advance this explanation still hold, however, that the poltergeist haunting can only take place if the spirit involved is able to draw physical energy from susceptible mortals, and here again adolescents are often thought to be the most likely targets.

Poltergeist disturbances are not as rare as one might suppose. I have investigated a number of such cases myself, and have been surprised at how many people, when hearing of my experiences, recount inexplicable events that have taken place in their own homes. Many of these can probably be put down to natural causes (including the all too physical activity of mischievous children!), but a sizeable residue seem inexplicable by normal means, and the subject must remain open to further debate and research.

MAGIC

We cannot leave a chapter that has touched upon ESP and poltergeists without some reference to the subject of magic itself. And by magic I mean not stage conjurors, but those curious beliefs prevalent down the centuries that men and women, by the use of spells and rituals, can directly influence the workings of the natural world. Children are firm believers in magic, not only because they encounter it so often in films and stories but also because the world is still such a mysterious place for them that it is easy to believe that almost anything can happen. Naturally enough, as they grow older they will begin to have doubts, and will demand to know whether magic *really* exists.

The answer is not quite as straightforward as it might seem. Science appears to have banished magic to the level of primitive superstition, yet travellers in South America, in India, in Africa and in other places where communities live close to nature still come across well-authenticated tales of mysterious happenings beyond the understanding of the modern rational mind, including apparently miraculous examples of physical and psychological healing. I have myself met many such tales on my own travels in these lands, and it is important that we do not prematurely close the minds of our children to the possible existence of forces outside the currently known laws of the universe. The apparent existence of ESP is a potent reminder that there are many laws that still remain to be discovered.

Magic is essentially about transformation. Only rarely was it the intention of the magician to gain power over others. Usually he or she sought for power over the self and over the forces of nature in order to bring about spiritual transformation, or to effect healing transformations in the body, or to ensure the transformation of infertile land to fertile. Much of the effectiveness of magic came from the united, positive thinking of the whole community. If everyone shares a single, unshakeable belief that the crops will thrive, then the combined power of this thinking may indeed help to bring about the desired outcome. This is no different from the current belief, to which organized Western religion still at least pays lip-service, of the power of prayer. Modern findings that plants that receive water blessed by a faith healer thrive in comparison to those which do not, provide some practical support for beliefs of this kind.

Religion and magic have always been inextricably mixed, in that religious faith and practices have been deemed to bring about deep inner transformations. In the East it has long been accepted that progress in meditation and in the more esoteric forms of yoga can lead to the development of magical powers (*siddhis* as they are properly called), and the practitioner is always counselled against their use except in the strict service of others. For example, in the Tibetan Buddhist and the Hindu traditions, the master is sometimes said to visit the pupil during the sleep and dreams of the latter, and to impart spiritual teachings of particular power. I have myself talked to monks and nuns who have been in receipt of such teachings. The master is also said to be able to open the 'third eye' of spiritual wisdom in the pupil, and to remain in telepathic contact with him or her over vast distances.

If magic of this kind does exist, people often ask whether it can be used for evil ends as well as for good. Black magic features not infrequently in the stories of children, and from time to time accounts of satanic rituals involving child abuse surface in the popular press. The major distinction that has always been drawn between black magic of this kind and the more exalted forms of magic associated with spirituality is that the former is concerned primarily to gain power for oneself, whereas the latter is interested only in the service of others. The human mind contains many mysteries, and if emotional energy can be concentrated and directed outwards, then – just like any other energies – it can be used to serve undesirable as well as desirable ends. Any accounts given by children of black magic (whether associated with particular cults or not) should therefore always be listened to with due attention. Usually they boil down to no more than the fears and fantasies children delight to spread among themselves, or to fictional stories that have mistakenly been read as fact. But occasionally there may be some element of truth in these accounts, and they may have to be reported to the police or social services so that the children concerned be properly protected.

DREAMS AND DREAMING

Dreams allow us each night to enter the most extraordinary fantasy world, in which we become players in magical dramas of such intensity that they may for a time seem more real than waking life. In dreams we fly unaided, walk through walls, meet people long dead, roam the silent corridors of strange mansions, flee from monsters, ride on mythical beasts, meet the gods, experience our own deaths and resurrections, and generally taste the infinite possibilities of the human mind. Research indicates that we each appear to dream every night, usually in five or six progressively longer cycles, with the last of them occupying anything between 20 and 40 minutes. People who say they never have dreams probably simply fail to remember them. In sleep laboratories, where subjects are awoken each time their brain patterns indicate they have entered the level of sleep where dreaming usually takes place, virtually everyone reports a dream of some kind.

Young children are particularly vivid dreamers, although the *content* of their dreams (not surprisingly in view of their more limited life experience) is usually more limited than that of adults. Naturally they ask parents what dreams are for, particularly as a high percentage of their dreams may be frightening or actively terrifying. The answer, even after many centuries of speculation, and many hours of scientific investigation in more recent decades, is that we are still not sure. Theories abound, but there is no single one that is accepted as valid by all psychologists.

However, during sleep the conscious mind becomes de-activated, and the unconscious takes over and weaves its subtle stories and pictures. Thus the most likely theory is that dreams are the language of the unconscious, and reveal aspects of ourselves that are usually beyond the reach of our waking thought. Carl Jung, one of the leading authorities on dreams and their meaning, once said that we probably dream 24 hours of the day, but that in waking life dream images are kept out of our awareness by the constant chatter of the conscious mind. Only in sleep are they able to make their presence felt.

To understand the meaning of dreams, we must recognize that they are rarely what they seem. The unconscious mind operates in a symbolic rather than a rational way. Sigmund Freud, another major authority on dreams, suggested this was in order to disguise dream content from the conscious mind, lest the latter, outraged by certain aspects of this content, would rouse itself from sleep and put a stop to the dreaming process. Jung suggested, however, that the unconscious operates symbolically because it is older and wiser than the rational, linguistic, conscious mind, and connects us at a deep level not only to the minds of other living people (one possible explanation for telepathy) but also to the whole history of the human race. Symbols, whether in the form of shapes, of symbolic events and characters, or of the ancient gods, are thus expressions of the fundamental psychological and spiritual energies that make us human and motivate us to seek for meaning and purpose in existence.

On this interpretation, dreams are ways of putting us in touch not only with the anxieties and the needs and aspirations of our personal history but also with those of the whole human race. By studying our dreams and unravelling their meaning, we thus come not only better to understand ourselves but also to understand our eternal destiny as men and women. It is impossible to explain all this to very young children, but it does lead us to two important conclusions, firstly, that even the weirdest and apparently nonsensical dreams carry a hidden meaning and, secondly, that this meaning is to be taken seriously.

In the case of young children, this means that we should listen carefully to their dreams, never laugh at or ridicule what they tell us about them, and never dismiss this information as 'only a dream'. Children who suffer particularly from nightmares are indicating to us that there are frightening experiences in their waking lives with which they have not been able as yet to come to terms. These may be associated with the strength of their own emotions, or with the fears aroused in them by the powerful adults in their lives. If a child is consistently misunderstood or punished by adults for expressions of emotion, he or she may come to see these emotions as evil forces lurking deep inside the self and ready to break out and overwhelm conscious attempts at controlling them and at being 'good' and thus worthy of parental love and acceptance (see Chapter 2). Fears of powerful adults may be aroused not only by punitive parental behaviour but also by the sheer size of grown-ups as compared to small children. Adults tower above children, and can often startle them quite unintentionally by swift movements, loud voices and so on. Unable to equate the role of parents and adults as the givers of love and protection with their role as the bringers of fear and suffering (an issue also dealt with in Chapter 2), children repress the latter role deep into their unconscious, where it emerges symbolically in dreams.

The analysis of childhood dreams suggests that giants and monsters may thus often symbolize the punitive, terrifying father, while witches may symbolize the punitive, frightening mother. Even children who have excellent relationships with their parents may have dreams featuring these distressing characters from time to time, as they may also represent other adults, or those occasions even in the calmest of households where parents startle children with sudden displays of firmness or annoyance.

Although an unpleasant experience at the time, nightmares thus fulfil a useful psychological function. They allow repressed fears to come to the surface, thus dissipating the bottled-up emotional energy concerned, and they also alert us to the fact that certain waking experiences may be having more of an impact upon the child than we had realized, and may need rather different handling in the future. Young children cannot be protected from all the fears and upsets that are a part of life. Indeed it would not be a good thing if they could, since they have to adjust emotionally to the challenges that the world will inevitably present to them in the years to come. But if the dream-life of young children indicates that they are experiencing fears and terrors that are beyond the capacity of their immature years to handle, then we must look very carefully at the environment that we are providing for them. As adults we must keep in mind that children do not choose their own environment. They are almost completely at the mercy of their elders in this respect, and their elders thus carry a particular sacred trust in the matter.

Of course, much of children's dreaming is very pleasant, and they should be encouraged to talk about this as well, since it will also carry useful symbolic messages of one kind or another. There is no need to probe too deeply into these messages, as the main thing in these early years to to help the child develop a life-long habit of remembering and learning from dreams. But all dream interpretation depends upon identifying the symbolic meaning that dreams contain, and this is best done by taking the most striking dream images or events, and seeing what associations or ideas they suggest. A young child can be asked 'What does that make you think about?' in connection with these images or events, and the likely meaning of the dream allowed to emerge as a result.

Sometimes this meaning will be to do with the child's hopes or expectations, sometimes to do with things that may have happened the previous day but that have not been properly understood, or that have aroused special emotions (pleasant or otherwise). Sometimes it will have to do with the child's wish for adventure or excitement (though even here the *nature* of the adventure or excitement portrayed in the dream can tell us a great deal about the child), sometimes with apprehensions about the future, sometimes with the problems and curiosities faced by his or her waking mind. But whatever the meaning concerned, it must be treated with respect and – it goes without saying – the child never made to feel worried or guilty about his or her dream content.

Paying attention to children's dreams is often a good way to arouse interest once more in our own. Almost all cultures prior to that of modern Western man have taken dreams seriously. Many of the world's great scriptures (including the Bible) refer to divine wisdom coming in the form of dreams. The ancient Egyptians, Babylonians, Greeks and Romans all saw dreams as telling the future, while for many centuries they have also been regarded as giving clues to physical illness and its cures. In the time of the ancient Greeks individuals with problems of one kind or another used to sleep in the temple (after taking a special potion of herbs), and offer their dreams in the morning to the priest for interpretation. In many cultures (including the shamanic cultures of Asia and of the Americas) the soul is believed to leave the body during sleep and travel in the astral and other realms. Tibetan Buddhists have a particular practice of dream yoga, in which the individual is trained to remain conscious throughout dreaming, so that dreams can be used to visit one's teacher and listen to his or her teachings. Since in Tibetan Buddhism sleep is regarded as a nightly dress rehearsal for death, it is also considered that dreams can give insights into the after-death state, and allow the dreamer, when the time comes, to die in full consciousness and thus control what happens in this state. And as already mentioned, even in our materialistic society, many eminent psychologists believe that dreams can give invaluable insights into our psychological lives.

Often when talking about their dreams, children want to hear about adults' dream experiences too. This not only confirms their intuitive feeling that dreams are important and meaningful but it also allows them (even without dream interpretation) to come to know more about their parents' inner lives. For a child it is enormously interesting to know that a father dreams sometimes about long train journeys, or about finding himself naked in public, or about standing up to give a lecture and finding he can't remember what he is supposed to say, and to know that a mother dreams about riding up into the sky on a magnificent white horse, or of swimming in a rough sea or of getting arrested inside a large department store and wrongly accused of shop-lifting. The essential humanity of their parents becomes particularly obvious to children when listening to such dream accounts of adult anxieties, fallibilities and aspirations, while the accounts themselves give parents and children the opportunity to laugh together (a not inconsiderable aid towards good parent–child relationships!).

Sharing dreams with their children gives adults the incentive to start remembering their dreams again (something that may not have happened for years), and to begin to search them for meaning. Dreams are best remembered, firstly, through the simple decision to take them seriously, and to tell the mind as it drifts into sleep to recall them upon awakening and, secondly, by keeping a notebook beside the bed so that anything that is recalled can be written down before it starts to fade. By associating the themes, characters and experiences in dreams in the manner already described, we can then begin to identify those aspects of our mental and emotional lives that may need attention, either to lay the hidden fears (some of them left over from childhood) to rest, or to encourage those aspects of ourselves that the dream is telling us have hitherto been neglected. On occasions we may recall what

Jung called *grand dreams*, those dreams that appear to have a numinous, cosmic quality, and that once recalled stay in the conscious mind for years to come. These dreams may involve meeting an archetypal figure (for example, a wise old man or woman, a hero or god-like figure, a beautiful young woman) who imparts a profound message of some kind, or who uplifts and inspires simply by their presence.

Alternatively the grand dream may contain an archetypal event, such as the search for a secret treasure, or a journey through a dark forest, or a triumphant battle with the forces of evil. But whatever the form of the dream, it relates to the higher, spiritual side of our nature, which like other aspects of our inner life may have become buried and neglected over the years. The dream gives a clear indication that we must open ourselves once more to this side of our being, and to the higher meaning and purpose that it brings to life. Carl Jung reported that of the people who came to him in psychotherapy, the problem from middle life onwards was always a religious one – that is it had to do with a search for something in existence that lay beyond the immediate and the material, however successful the individuals concerned may have been in their everyday lives.

In children, the spiritual side of life, the sense of mystery and awe and of some great hidden purpose working in their lives and in the world around them, is much nearer the surface than it is for the most part in adulthood. Dreaming is one of the keys to this aspect of being. By helping our children to remain in contact with their dream-life we help them to keep their spirituality undimmed. And by re-activating our dream life in response to theirs, we help to remove some of the veil that over the years has served to come between us and our own vision.

CHAPTER 9

The Child at School

The start of formal schooling is a particular watershed in the lives of both young children and their parents. For children it is a major step in that widening of horizons that will eventually take them into the adult world, and for parents it is a an inevitable part of the process of loosening the ties of dependence between their children and themselves. These two issues are best discussed separately.

STARTING SCHOOL

A child's world is a small world, bounded by the familiar and the known: the house and garden, the local shops, parents, grandparents and siblings, neighbours and close friends, toys and books. These combine to give the child a sense of comfort and security. The world is manageable and comprehensible, made safe by parents and by the comfort of much-loved possessions. But when the time comes to start school, all this changes. Most adults experience starting a new job from time to time, and having to adapt to new surroundings, new demands and responsibilities, and new colleagues, but this is as nothing compared to the child's transition from home to school. In one short day the child exchanges the familiar for the unfamiliar, the predictable for the unpredictable, the safe for the uncertain, and however carefully he or she may have been prepared for the change, it is never short of emotionally demanding, and in some cases can border on the traumatic.

Among the many changes that the child faces, there is an abrupt change in self-identity. Within the home young children come to recognize themselves in terms of their relationship with their parents. The praise, encouragement and support received from parents give them good feelings about themselves, and help in the development of a confident and positive self-image. In general, they know what is wanted and expected of them, and know they are able to measure up to it. Now suddenly their parents are replaced during the day by teachers, new and very powerful adults who may have a quite different approach to relationships, and whose attitude towards them may have many dissimilarities from that of their parents. Small wonder that many children become confused. Previously they thought of themselves as loved and respected and at the centre of things, now they find themselves treated much less personally, reprimanded in ways that never happen at home, and called upon to share adult attention with large numbers of other children.

At the same time, these other children may also pose problems. They may have quite different standards of behaviour, or may appear much more competent in performing classroom tasks, or may be openly hostile and rejecting. In the midst of it all, the small child may lose sight of who he or she is, and become increasingly insecure and fretful. Children are adaptable people, and most of them eventually settle into the new routine and the new self-image that goes with it, but the shock of starting school can in some cases cause emotional wounds that are slow to heal, and that leave feelings of insecurity and unworthiness that can last for many years to come. Should the child be exposed to repeated experiences of failure within the school system itself, these feelings can be particularly persistent and damaging.

Experience of nursery school and pre-school playgroup can give a child something of the taste of things to come, as can visits to the new school, and friendly meetings with the teacher and with future classmates. Most schools are much better these days at initiating a child gently into formal education. Some even allow half-day attendance at first, and the presence of parents in the classroom during the early days. But in the end children have to be fully absorbed into school life, and become part of an environment in which they have far less control over their own lives than they have at home. And here they face another potential upset. Up to now their parents have usually been the supreme authorities in their lives, exercising unquestioned power to protect them from the outside world. Now suddenly children see this power taken from their parents. At the time when they want a mother or a father most, they find themselves apparently abandoned to the superior authority of the school. Parents must do as the teacher tells them, even to the extent of handing them over at the school gate and going home without them. In a sense, many children feel that the trust they have learned to place in their parents (Chapter 3) has been betrayed, and that the world has suddenly become a colder and more intimidating place.

It is small wonder that children often become difficult at home during the first weeks and months of schooling. At the end of the school day they feel a particular need to re-assert themselves within the home, and to demand attention from parents who they somehow feel have let them down by sending them to school. If there are brothers or sisters below school age, they may resent the fact they have been allowed to stay home all day and have undivided parental attention, and there may be angry jealous scenes in consequence. In addition, the child may have had particular problems at school during the day, with the teacher or with other children or with assigned tasks, and may want to vent their frustration or emotional upset upon others. Young children are rarely able to talk about these problems, and express them through actions rather than through words. To cap it all, they are often tired, hungry, and full of real or imagined fears about what may happen at school the next day.

Parents who understand their child's state of mind at these times are usually much better able to cope. The child is not deliberately trying to make life difficult for everyone just for the sake of it, but is in the grip of very confused and powerful emotions. He or she has to learn that the standards and values of the home must still be respected, and that certain forms of behaviour are unacceptable, whatever the reason, but his or her need for reassurance and love, and for some space in which to let off steam, are vitally important. If the home is still to be seen as a place where the child is loved and understood, and where people are allowed to be themselves and express their feelings, then parental reactions during these critical moments when the child is making the transition from school back to home are of major importance. Stern unaccepting parenting, and frequent battles of wills, only show children that there is now no place in the world where they can feel safe and happy.

LEARNING TO READ

Of course, once they become reconciled to school, most children enjoy the experience. They welcome the interest and stimulation involved, the opportunity to make new friends and play new games, and the feeling of being more grown-up. Provided there is no major clash of values between the two, they also find that home and school reinforce each other, and combine to provide the knowledge and skills that help them learn the all-important lesson of competence referred to in Chapter 3. The closer the ties between home and school, the more potent this reinforcement will become. These ties are forged by parents who take a ready interest in the child's schooling, who provide help and encouragement wherever possible, and who themselves have the knowledge needed to supplement what the child learns from the teacher.

One of the most important areas of this knowledge is learning to read. I have already discussed the value of reading to children, and of stimulating their imagination and their understanding through stories (Chapter 3). Any time between the ages of around 3 to 7 years children begin to show an interest in learning to read for themselves, and although the school plays a major role in developing this interest, the home can be of even greater importance. It is unfortunate that the teaching of reading has become surrounded by such an involved mystique that many parents feel they are unqualified to play any part in it. Nothing could be further from the truth.

Learning to read involves three prime ingredients. One interested child, one suitable book, and one patient adult. Given these three ingredients, any child without a major learning disability will master the skills of reading, and do so moreover with an enjoyment that will help sow the seeds of a life-long love of books. Learning to read has its beginnings in being read to. The child who is read to (initially in very short spells but for longer periods as his or her concentration span lengthens) from the second year of life onwards, soon comes to associate books – and the strange marks on the printed page – with pleasure. Almost from the beginning, the adult reading to the child should point to each word as it is pronounced, so that the child comes naturally to associate each word with a separate sound. Many children become so familiar with the idea that they start to 'read' the words of oft-repeated stories along with the adult, and can be encouraged to point at the words for themselves as the story goes along.

The next step is to obtain the first book in a high quality reading series. Preferably, the one used by the school that the child will attend (or is already attending) should be used. Some schools actively encourage children to take their reading books home with them for this purpose, but if this isn't the case the book can be ordered from any good book shop. The adult then reads page one to the child, and suggests the child might like to try the opening lines for him- or herself. No attempt is made to force the issue. If the child shows reluctance, this usually means he or she is not yet ready for the experience, and the book can be put aside for a time and re-introduced when the child has matured a little.

However, either now or a little later, the child will take up the adult's suggestion, and from now on the golden rule for teaching reading consists of three simple words: *pause, cue, prompt*. This means that when the child meets a word that cannot be recognized (initially this may be every word) the adult pauses for a moment to give the child sufficient opportunity to remember it if possible, then if nothing is said cues the child by giving the initial sound of the word, and if still nothing is said, prompts the child by reading the whole word, which the child is then asked to repeat. After a line of print has been covered in this way, the child can be invited to re-read the whole line.

It is vital that this whole process is carried out in a relaxed, even playful way. The child should never be scolded for not recognizing a word, even though it may have been encountered earlier on the same page, and the adult should never show any sign of impatience or frustration. The truth is that the child will read the word *if he or she can*. No child of this age will deliberately pretend to be obtuse in order to anger the adult. If the child doesn't read the word, it is because the word as yet can't be recognized. It will come in due course.

Equally importantly, no reading session should go on longer than the child can sustain interest and concentration. As soon as the child shows signs of wanting to stop, the book should be put on one side. Under no circumstances should he or she be made to associate learning to read with stress and boredom. Reading in these early years must always be for enjoyment.

Once the child has begun to master a number of words, he or she can be asked to pick out similar words lower down the page. The adult can help if necessary by pointing to these words and asking the child to say whether they are the same or not. Initially, children learn to read by recognizing the overall shape of a word, but as they progress, the adult can begin to split words into their constituent sounds, thus allowing the child to see that individual letters or combinations of letters represent separate sounds. This then helps them to tackle new words made up of these sounds, though here again the adult must never assume that the child will necessarily recognize these first time. The adult should pause-cue-prompt in the usual way, remind the child where these sounds occurred earlier on, and then proceed to the next word.

Naturally the child will spot quite early on that there are certain irregularities about the way in which we pronounce the words of the English language. He or she should be praised for recognizing this, and informed that at one time people used to pronounce words very much more closely to their spelling, but that over the years pronunciation changes. Provided they are given time and encouragement and appropriate reminders, most children experience few difficulties in mastering the anomalies concerned.

A good series of reading books contains a phased input of new words, and a controlled repetition of familiar ones. Thus the child is not asked to do too much too soon, and is also given regular practice in words that have already been learned. The vocabulary used in the books also contains a rising level of difficulty, and introduces children progressively to what are known as the *key words to literacy*, that is the words most frequently used in everyday speech.

In learning any skill and in any area of development, children tend to proceed at an uneven pace. A period of little apparent progress will be followed by a period of rapid progress, followed by another slower period. During these quiet periods it seems as if the child is consolidating what has already been learned, and only when this consolidation is complete is he or she ready for the next leap forward. Fallow periods are therefore no cause for anxiety, and certainly no cause for conveying any anxiety to the child. Learning in young children always takes place best in an atmosphere of interest, of low stress levels, and of support and encouragement. The child needs to know that the adult has every confidence that he or she is capable of the learning concerned, and will soon master it given the right opportunity. The adult's own interest in the task being undertaken is also important. In the case of reading, this means makes reference during the session to 'I wonder what happens next?', 'I'm excited to know what they are going to do' and so on.

Pictures also are a great help. Many children like to look forward in a book, and to talk about the pictures and speculate on the events associated with them. This is all to the good, and time spent talking about pictures, questioning the child on the details contained in them, and providing verbal descriptions of these details is time well spent. It helps bring the book to life and motivate the child to read on, and also provides some (often much needed!) variety for the adult.

Most teachers welcome the help given to the child by parents. In a large class of twenty children or more, the teacher cannot hope to hear each child read every day, and the presence of good readers in the class allows him or her to spend more time with those children who really need assistance. There is usually no fear of good readers being held back by a teacher reluctant to allow them to proceed at their own pace. Some schools actually hold classes for parents on how they can co-operate with the school in the teaching of reading and of other basic skills, and recognize that the more communication and liaison between parents and teachers on educational matters the better. In such cases few conflicts are likely to arise between home and school, and the child's recognition of the close links between the two tends to give him or her an added sense of security.

OTHER EARLY LEARNING SKILLS

I have placed particular emphasis upon helping the child learn to read not only because of the great importance of reading in the modern world but also because it is a way of bringing parent and child even closer together. To help a child to read is one of the most precious gifts that a parent can give, and also allows the parent to feel closely and importantly involved in the new voyage of discovery upon which the child is embarking with the coming of formal education. But there are also many other areas on which parents can assist their children. Practice in number skills (addition and subtraction, and later multiplication and division) are an obvious example, but here it is particularly important that the school be consulted first. There are many different methods for teaching early number work to children, and children can become very confused if the school and the home differ in their approach. Some schools use work cards that they prepare themselves instead of relying upon written text books, and it is obviously vital that parents know about these and understand the principles upon which they are based.

Spelling is another area in which parents can be of great help. Educational fashions in regard to spelling tend to change, just as do fashions in the teaching of reading and of number work. At one time, spelling was regarded as of great importance, and many children were made to suffer deeply and unnecessarily over their difficulties in this area. The teaching of spelling then fell into disrepute, as it was recognized by educationalists that concern over getting words right often inhibited children in word use during their creative writing. Currently, the pendulum has swung back somewhat, and the teaching of spelling (albeit without the dreaded spelling tests of yesteryear) is again receiving some attention.

Many children who read well have difficulty with spelling, simply because their precocity in reading means that they do not pause long enough to notice the internal construction of words (whether 'i ' comes before 'e' and so on). Other children have difficulties caused by some perceptual disability. They literally cannot recognize and hold in their minds the appearance of words (as in so-called dyslexic children). Whatever the reason for the difficulties, spelling should never be made a big issue between adults and children. Practice, plus an introduction to the few spelling rules that exist, is the most important way of helping a child, together with a reminder occasionally to read a page slowly and spend a little time looking at how each individual word is put together.

In addition to the basic skills, children need help in developing a wide range of other interests. Many of these arise in response to direct experience. It is a mistake to assume that children will develop their various enthusiasms spontaneously. For the most part, they need first to be exposed to the appropriate stimuli, which then help arouse their latent potential. No child, whatever his or her latent gifts, will become a musician unless he or she is exposed to music. No child will become an artist unless exposed to art, and no child will become a sports star unless exposed to sport. Parents who care about such things see to it that their children are taken on visits to museums, cathedrals, country houses, picture galleries, theatres, concerts, and anything else likely to capture their imagination. Provided the child is not 'expected' to be immediately enraptured, or to linger beyond his or her attention span, such outings can be a source of great pleasure for all the family. The better informed parents are, and the more able to answer the child's stream of questions, the more likely is it that the experiences concerned will leave a lasting impression upon his or her mind.

Similarly, children need scope to follow up their interests within the home. The more access they have to the facilities and equipment needed to feed their interests, the more likely are these to become fruitful and enduring. To parents who object about the 'mess' that a child's interests can create within the home, my answer is that it is the child's home just as much as it is the home of the parents. Failure to allow him or her – within reasonable limits – to treat it as such is a recipe for disaster later on. Parents who complain that their adolescent sons and daughters treat the home as an hotel are usually the very parents who never allowed their children when young to feel that the home belonged to them. Small wonder that many such children have little regard for it later on, and can hardly wait until they can leave and have a place that they can really call their own.

Childish interests and a certain degree of mess are inseparable. I invariably worry when I enter a house containing young children and find no evidence of their existence. Why aren't I falling over toys I wonder, or having to remove books or crayonings from a chair before sitting down? Why aren't there jam jars full of sprouting seeds and living things on the windowsills, childish paintings and drawings on the walls, and signs of enthusiastic baking and cooking in the kitchen? Why are there no musical instruments on view, no puzzles, no paste pots, no games, no general clutter, no climbing frames or swings or footballs in the garden? Homes that are geared solely to the convenience of adults are hardly suitable places for young children, and definitely not recommended for the nurturing and development of young children's talents and interests.

One of the great pleasures of parenthood is entering fully into the world of the child, and developing new enthusiasms along with him or her. It is extraordinary how one's horizons can open out in company with those of one's children, and it is sad when a parent has no time to spare to nurture their interests. Like a good teacher, one of the signs of a good parent is that however busy he or she may be, he or she is always able to find this time. In one sense it is a question of priorities. If parenting comes high on the list, then no matter how pressing other commitments may be, the child is never expected to take a back seat. Parents who worry that this may mean the child is always demanding attention can be reassured. It is the child who is neglected who develops strategies (including misbehaviours of various kinds) for gaining attention. Children who know that parents are always available to them are far more likely to wait for a more appropriate time when they see parents are busy with other things. The reassuring knowledge that parents will always turn to you when you really want them is the best way to help a child develop real consideration about the demands he or she decides to make.

INTEREST SPAN AND SEX-RELATED DIFFERENCES

However much enthusiasm a child shows for a new interest, there is no guarantee that it is going to last. Some children have much shorter interest spans than others, and with any child, enthusiasms wax and wane. It is a great mistake to rush out and spend a great deal of money supporting a child's interest right at the outset, and then to blame him or her if the interest disappears and the money seems to have been wasted. Attempts to harass the child into maintaining the interest only makes things worse. Sometimes it may spontaneously resurrect later on, just as often it may not. But children cannot turn their interests on and off to suit parents, and the best plan of action is to encourage the child without exaggerating the investment of capital. Later, when it is clear that the interest is likely to be long-term, things will be different, but initially even children with lengthy interest spans are experimenting with each new enthusiasm. Until they become involved in it, even they have no idea how deep their liking for it is going to go, and if they find this liking soon begins to fade, at least they have added to their store of knowledge about the world and about themselves.

One question that parents often ask has to do with differences in interests between boys and girls. Are the sexes drawn towards different things even from an early age, and if so is this a consequence of nature or nurture? The answer is that genetic differences between boys and girls do seem to be apparent from an early age. There is of course a large overlap, with many girls liking boys' pursuits and vice versa, but boys generally seem more drawn towards robust physical activities and the outdoor life, and girls towards more thoughtful and indoor pursuits. Girls are generally more forward in language development and in reading and writing skills, while boys are more practical and may show more aptitude in mathematics and in the solution of spatial problems. In the years to come, there is some evidence that boys show a wider ability range than girls, with more boys in both the highly gifted and the slow learning category than girls, but too much should not be read into these differences, since educational opportunities also play a major part in determining them.

Environment in fact begins to play a part in sex-related differences from the very early years onwards. In two-parent households boys tend to identify with their father and girls with their mother, acquiring some of their interests accordingly. As boys are generally given more freedom than girls, they have more chance to play and learn outside the home, while girls have more opportunity to be with adults and to learn adult language skills. And as physical aggression is more countenanced in boys, girls have more incentive to acquire language in order to express themselves, and there is some evidence that they can be more verbally aggressive than boys. With the exception of self-assertion, girls are allowed more freedom than boys in expressing their emotions, and boys are often emotionally handicapped by being prevented from giving way to tears and from expressing their anxieties and the gentler side of their natures.

For parents, the best guidance is that opportunities should as far as possible be made equally available to boys and girls, and the children themselves left to decide what they prefer. In many cases girls will gravitate towards dolls and house play, while boys will go for cars and guns. It is unrealistic to try to go against this trend once it becomes developed. Whether for innate or for cultural reasons, that is the way in which the children concerned feel happiest and most in tune with their friends, and that is the way in which inevitably they will go, no matter how much encouragement they may be given to the contrary.

SCHOOL REFUSAL

Nearly all children show a reluctance to go to school from time to time. This may be because of an unpopular teacher, or of hostility or active bullying from other children, or the threat of a test or examination, or a dreaded subject on the timetable, or simply boredom or physical tiredness. It is important to take these reasons for wanting to stay at home seriously. Children have to go to school, and parents cannot allow them to stay at home just when they feel like it. But this very compulsion behind school attendance means that children deserve to be listened to when they have problems. If an adult dislikes a job, he or she can always, in the final analysis, decide to resign and look for something else. A child is not in this happy position. The attendant feelings of powerlessness can be very real and disturbing, and can only be lessened by a sympathetic adult ready to listen and to help sort out any problems that have arisen.

In many cases this will involve visiting the school and alerting teachers or headteachers to what the child appears to be going through. Most schools are only too ready to listen to parents, and to do all they can to protect children from undue anxiety and distress. But they are in no position to do so if they are simply unaware of what is happening. Parents are closer to their children than are teachers, and provided the child is always encouraged – without fear of censure or unfair criticism – to discuss school with parents, the latter are in the best position to know what troubles may be arising and why.

Very occasionally however, all attempts at meeting a child's fears and encouraging and supporting his or her schooling prove unsuccessful. The child simply refuses to go to school, and no amount of reasoning and persuading appears to help matters. Parents and teachers do everything they can but to no avail, and interventions from the school welfare officer and the school psychologist prove no more effective. One theory has it that at this point everyone should get tough. The child should be taken to school (in pyjamas if need be) by force, and kept there by similar means.

Few strategies could be more misguided. The child may indeed be forced into remaining in school by this means, but not only will this do little for his or her readiness (and ability) to profit from the experience but it will also destroy much of the relationship with parents and adults and leave deep psychological wounds. The child now has to face not only the problems that led to the school refusal in the first place but also the feelings of powerlessness and worthlessness attendant upon being forced there against his or her will.

Enlightened education authorities have special units for children who are recognized to have genuine terrors about attending school (school phobics at they are sometimes called). This is the only effective – and humane – way of gradually helping the child to overcome these terrors, and of providing educational experience at the same time. School phobics are usually desperately unhappy about their plight. They would much prefer to be able to go to school along with other children. In a significant number of cases it proves impossible (as sometimes happens with other phobias in adults and in children) even to identify the exact reasons for their fears. The child may be as mystified by them as everyone else. They could be related to an early traumatic experience of some kind at school, which has now been buried in the child's unconscious. Or they could be related to associations set off by the school that link to traumas in other areas of life (deep insecurities, feelings of being unloved or rejected, an obscure dread that parents will 'disappear' while the child is at school). Whatever the reason, the only approach is through patience and understanding. We would never brutally (and against his or her will) thrust an adult phobic back into the very conditions that cause the phobia to arise, and there is no excuse for attempting to do so with a child.

WHERE SCHOOLS FAIL CHILDREN

As indicated earlier, schools may fail children by giving them insufficient opportunities to experience success. In fact it is no exaggeration to say that our Western educational system is often much better at producing failures than at producing successes. Far too many children leave school with little in the way of formal qualifications, and little in the way of the skills they will need if they are to make their way in life.

Schools can also inhibit children's creativity (Chapter 6) by instilling in them such a morbid fear of making mistakes that they eschew the risk-taking in ideas and in performance so essential for creative endeavour. Too often the 'right' answer is the one in the textbook or in the teacher's head, and the child is not encouraged to question, to doubt, or to come up with his or her own way of looking at things.

But our educational system fails children in a number of other important ways, connected this time with the actual curriculum. Schools teach children very little about human relationships (including sexual relationships), about the use and control of the emotions, about self-understanding, about psychological health, about spirituality, about identifying life goals and personal values, and virtually nothing at all about training the mind. This last may sound paradoxical, as we frequently hear the claim that education 'trains the mind'. In fact it does nothing of the sort. It restricts itself to training the child how to use information, and although it often does this very effectively, there is a world of difference between this and training the mind.

Mind training involves an understanding of the workings of one's own mind, a degree of control over thinking so that the mind can still the internal chatter and relax properly, an ability to focus and concentrate the attention instead of being lost in distractions, an ability to organize and manage time, to improve the memory, and to bring a level of efficiency to the workings of the mind that without such training usually remains way beyond most of us. These issues are so important that they are returned to in more detail in Chapter 10.

LETTING CHILDREN GO

I mentioned at the beginning of the chapter that when children start school, parents as well as the children themselves are faced with something of a watershed, because starting school involves loosening the ties of dependence. Some parents welcome this, and see the coming of school as an opportunity to concentrate more on other commitments and interests, such as a career outside or inside the home. But for many parents the day when a child begins school carries a special poignancy, because from now on they see their child as moving progressively further away from them. The era of early childhood is passed, and from now on other adults will increasingly influence the child, make demands on him or her, and have rights over his or her time and attention and behaviour. Other children will also feature more prominently in the child's life, and other interests in which parents may have little place will begin to develop.

Starting school is in fact a rite of passage, and from now on parenthood involves that process of letting go that culminates in the moment when children finally leave home to start their independent lives. The ease with which we can let go of our children has a lot to do with the extent to which our identity is bound up with them. Many parents devote their lives, not only in terms of love and service but also in terms of concepts and self-image, to their children, and not surprisingly find great difficulty in accepting the fact that one day these children outgrow the home and want to make their own way in the world. Such parents feel diminished when this time arrives, and sometimes admit to deep feelings of resentment, as if their child is wilfully and ungratefully throwing away all they have done for him or her.

It is natural and healthy that we should miss our children, first when they begin formal schooling, then when they move from the small world of the primary school into the much less personal one of the secondary school, and finally when they leave to go to university or to work away from home or to get married. If we have shared time and interests with them, as a good parent should, we are faced with doing things that we once did with our children on our own or with other adults.

However, in spite of this inevitable sadness, we should be free to experience pleasure in seeing our children ready to broaden their horizons and claim their independence. If the childhood years have gone well, we should also be free to experience pride in their achievements, and satisfaction in a parental job well done.

In order to experience this kind of freedom, I always counsel parents not to let too much of their identity become bound up with being a father or a mother, and certainly not to live too much of their lives and their interests through their children. Having dependent children is a temporary phase in life, and there are many other things in addition to this that define us as human beings.

Accepting this does not mean loving or enjoying our children any the less. Far from it. It allows us to see their lives as encompassing the years at home and the independent years that are to follow. As they grow older it also allows us more easily to change our relationship with them, so that we move progressively from a position of guidance and leadership to one of partnership and equality. The years pass too quickly, and soon our children may be cleverer, better qualified, and more successful in running their lives than are we in running ours. Throughout their formative years we have as much to learn from them as they have from us, and when they reach adulthood we may find ourselves having even more.

One way of looking at it is to recognize that the best way of keeping our children is to let them go. Should we try to hang on too tightly, then if they have any real spirit they will fight hard to break free. Should we on the other hand allow them to gain in independence and self-responsibility as the years go by, then they will always be enthusiastic about coming home and remaining part of the very close family. In a real sense we never lose them, and may even find that our relationship with them becomes more and more rewarding with the passage of time.

In addition to not investing too much of our identity in our children, we should also not make emotional demands upon them that ideally should only be made of another adult. This is perhaps a particular danger in single-parent families, or in families where one partner feels unfulfilled in his or her relationship with the other. The child is then expected to give a form of emotional warmth and support to the parent that is beyond him or her to give. Children in this position are in a very real sense never allowed emotionally to be children at all, and must study the feelings and sensitivity of a parent in the manner of a lover and not of that of a son or daughter. It is particularly difficult for a parent who feels lonely and vulnerable to avoid making such demands of a child, or for a parent who has an emotional need for qualities (strength, gentleness or whatever) that cannot be found in a partner. Yet unless we can avoid the danger, we place our child at considerable emotional risk, besides putting ourselves in a position where letting go becomes more difficult for us than ever.

CHAPTER 10

Body and Mind

LINKS BETWEEN BODY AND MIND

Modern psychology accepts the enormous importance of the links between body and mind. The spiritual traditions do not mislead us when they speak of the body as the temple of the spirit. And as befits a temple, the body must be honoured and cared for, and made suitable in every way for the spirit that it serves.

Honouring and respecting the body involve all the obvious things like good hygiene and nutrition, and a discussion of these lies outside the scope of this book. But it involves much more than these. It involves an acceptance and love of the body that has nothing to do with preening and vanity, and everything to do with a recognition of the marvels of the body, and with a gratitude for the loyal way in which it serves us during our lives.

Acceptance and love of this kind depend for their development upon a number of things. One of the most important is close and loving physical contact with parents and care-givers during the childhood years. Some children (known by child-care specialists as 'cuddlers') are much more drawn towards displays of physical affection than are others ('non-cuddlers'). But all children require a generous minimum of contact of this kind. Physical touch is a child's first language. Through it he or she becomes conscious of the love and care given by others, and through it he or she explores and learns about the world and its textures and surfaces. It is desperately hard for a child to learn the lesson of love (Chapter 4) without warm and gentle and intimate handling from parents and care-givers.

Very soon, touch takes on a further dimension of importance, in that it helps give the child the message that the body *per se* is physically attractive to others. Imagine the difference in body image between the child who is handled coldly and roughly (or worse still subjected to physical assault and abuse), and the child whose body is touched and handled only with gentleness and love. Objects we hold precious are always treated in the latter rather than the former way, and it is often the quality of the handling that conveys the sense of value more effectively than anything else. Psychological research has demonstrated that children with high self-esteem come most frequently from homes in which there is plenty of physical affection, and it is this physical affection, rather than the actual physical appearance of the children themselves, that determine the way in which they think about their bodies and develop their sense of personal worth.

It a sad fact of life that children with behaviour and/or personality problems characteristically take little real care of their bodies. Self-mutilation, drug abuse, over- or under-eating, poor nutrition, neglect of warning physical symptoms, and carelessness with personal safety are all features of children (and of adults) who come in these problem categories. They may at times exhibit an exaggerated over-preoccupation with their appearance, but this is linked almost always to external factors – such as a desire to attract the opposite sex – rather than to a genuine respect for their own persons.

Given a secure acceptance and liking for their own bodies, children then need reasoned guidance in bodily use. Young children have naturally good physical posture. By around the age of seven, with few exceptions they carry themselves with almost perfect balance. The lower back is straight, the spine is upright and the head held erect. When walking or running they move with a relaxed spontaneous grace, and even when sprawling on the floor their bodies arrange themselves with a minimum of strain and tension. Not only this, children delight in physical movement. They would as soon skip or hop or run as walk. Their energy appears boundless, and expresses much of their natural joy at being alive.

From the age of seven onwards however, we often see a decline in physical posture, culminating in the slouching, slumping of many an adolescent, and the increasingly cribbed and confined movements of the adult. Typically the head begins to jut forward instead of being held upright over the neck, the eyes begin to look downwards rather than upwards, the shoulders start to stoop, the hands are held awkwardly or plunged in the pockets, and the stride becomes jerky and unbalanced.

Why is this? Certainly it seems to be a particularly Western phenomenon. In most parts of India for example, and in Africa and the Far East, many people remain upright and graceful even into advanced old age. There is thus nothing programmed into the body to bring about its early postural deterioration. The answer would seem to lie in the mind. And indeed one only has to look at the cowed, dejected posture of people in deep depression (and of people with certain of the psychoses or mental illnesses) to witness the truth of this. If the mind feels bored or hopeless or generally out of tune with life, the body reflects it as faithfully as a mirror. And in the West we are indeed typically out of tune with life. We rarely walk if we can help it, and when we do our mind is not focused on the world around us but upon the chatter of our own thoughts. We have lost touch with nature, and rarely notice the blossom on the trees, or the shape of the clouds, or the beauty of the stars at night. Recently, to make matters worse, in adolescence we increasingly walk around with headphones clamped to our heads, lost in the trance-inducing rhythm of the latest in pop music.

We can learn so much from young children in the years before this decline sets in. I counsel parents to watch their young children, to note how they move, to register the way they hold themselves when in repose, to observe how each movement is an assent to life. I then suggest that they go upstairs and take a long, objective look at themselves in the mirror. Not so long ago, they were just like their own children. Where has that grace and suppleness gone? In profile, the stomach probably now hangs forward, the spine is alternatively hollowed and hunched, and the neck is dropped forward and the head pulled unnaturally back. In short, the body now in all probability increasingly resembles the shape of the letter 'S'.

My next suggestion to them is that they straighten the lower back by tilting the bottom of the pelvis forward, that they allow the spine to lengthen and the shoulders to straighten as a result, and that they then draw the head back so that it is once more carried upright. If they find all this too difficult, then instead I tell them simply to 'think up', as in the training associated with the Alexander Technique. When we 'think up', the body receives the message to straighten itself, and almost miraculously does just that. The body actually knows how to hold itself if given half a chance. The main problem is that the mind has for years been giving it the message to 'think down', and the more preoccupied the mind becomes with its own thoughts, the more insistently is this message given.

Once the body is allowed to 'think up', I ask people to note the difference this makes, not just in the body itself but in the mind. The very act of straightening the body, and allowing it to return to the posture that nature intended, gives a palpable lift to the spirits. People suffering with depression particularly notice the difference that improved posture makes, and often this can be a major factor in their return to a better frame of mind.

Re-educating the posture (or rather re-educating the mind in order to allow the posture to re-educate itself) takes time and trouble, and a close attention to both mind and body (much helped by the practice of meditation, discussed in more detail later in the chapter). It is much easier if one refrains from getting into bad habits in the first place. And here parents can help children both in direct and indirect ways. Direct ways involve reminding the child to pay more attention to posture once any signs of the adolescent slump begin to develop. Reminders of this kind should not degenerate into nagging or into a battle of wills however. The aim should be to motivate children to maintain the grace and beauty that is their birthright. Some children are well able to look ahead, and will easily appreciate the value in the coming years of body maintenance of this kind. Other children are more grounded in the moment, and will respond better to being praised for getting things right in the present.

Indirect ways involve encouraging the child from the very early years (for this and for many other very good reasons) to take an interest in nature and in their surroundings, to use eyes and ears and generally to look life in the face. Once upon a time children walked to school or rode on the tops of buses, now even though they may live no more than a stone's throw away they are as often as not taken by car. From my study window I see them each morning, typically slumped down in the back seat. Less and less do we encourage children to observe the world. More and more we encourage them to become passengers, and to pass through it without even noticing.

Indirect ways also involve help with mind training, and this is such an important issue that it is left until we discuss meditation later in the chapter.

MOVEMENT AND HEALTH

The value of physical exercise in the maintenance of both physical and psychological health is now too well-proven to be open to dispute. Appropriate physical exercise (guidelines vary somewhat, but 20 to 30 minutes of activity vigorous enough to drive the pulse rate to 80 per cent of its maximum four times a week represents a fair consensus) reduces the risk of heart disease and obesity, helps bodily metabolism and flexibility, and increases relaxation and feelings of well-being. There is some evidence that early signs of the damage within arteries that may lead to heart disease in later life is now apparent even in pre-adolescent children, and the theory is that this is due to a combination of inappropriate diet (too much sugar, salt and saturated animal fats, and too little fresh fruit and vegetables) and inadequate exercise.

It is estimated that at least one child in four fails to take sufficient exercise, thus storing up problems for the future, and that an equal number of children are over-weight. In many cases parents must take part of the blame. I mention above the number of children who are taken even a short distance to school by car, and to this can be added the number of children who are never taken on family walks, who never see their parents taking exercise, who are never bought games equipment, and who are over-provided with sedentary activities within the home (televisions and high-fi in bedrooms, computers, videos and video games, and so on). Human beings are composed of mind, body and soul, and unless all three are cared for and allowed to work in harmony, then some part of that humanity is being denied.

The secret of encouraging a life-long habit of physical exercise in children is – as with so many things – to start young. Children have a natural love of physical movement, as made clear above. From an early age (and with suitable support and encouragement) they can be taken swimming, to play ball in the park, to enjoy the swings in the local recreation ground, to ride their bicycles in safe areas, and to go for walks in the country. Provided the child is not allowed to become tired and bored, these early experiences, together with the pleasant associations thus built up of doing things as a family, will help to develop this love and ensure it survives into adult life. Equally, by taking part in these activities with their children, adults can experience once more the pleasures of physical exercise, and re-kindle some of their own enthusiasm for becoming and remaining physically fit.

Later on, the child can be encouraged to take part in organized games, both in school and with local clubs. The more skilled they become, the more children enjoy these experiences. It is untrue that organized games necessarily build character, but properly conducted they help a child relate socially and learn the value of team spirit, and to accept the feelings associated with both winning and losing. In setting the child a challenge of skill, they can also help in building self-confidence, and in learning to appreciate the skills of others, whether they happen to be ranged for or against one's own team.

DRESS AND APPEARANCE

Few children want to look different from their friends. In consequence their habits of dress and of appearance tend as they grow older to follow the latest craze. However, children who have a good body image, and who accept themselves both physically and psychologically, rarely resort to too many extremes. Whatever they wear they convey the impression of being clean and well-groomed, and of taking some pride in being who they are. Children who need to make a great show of projecting their personalities through the way in which they dress or style their hair are often rather unsure of themselves and of their identity. Similarly children who need to use their appearance to rebel against the standards of the adult world are doubtful of their ability to do so by more rational and convincing means.

In my experience parents quarrel with their children – particularly with their adolescent children – over clothes almost as frequently as they quarrel with them over tidiness. Such quarrels rarely bring about a change in child behaviours, and serve primarily to sour relationships between the generations, at least temporarily. Wise parents accept that children want to dress in a way acceptable to their friends, and also that they want to experiment with their appearance during the adolescent years, intent on identifying how they are going to look as adults. Little is therefore to be gained by trying too hard to make them conform to the standards of dress of their elders. And wise parents also accept that the quickest way for children to work through this stage of their development is to give them a reasonable amount of freedom. Failure to do so only prompts children to feel they are misunderstood, and to confirm them in the need to rebel against the adult world in order to claim the right to their own identity.

As in many differences of opinion with children, disagreements over clothes and over fashions also provide us as parents with an opportunity to re-examine some of our own prejudices. Fashions change in clothing and hairstyle and other aspects of physical appearance more rapidly than in anything else. What was considered unacceptable a few years ago is considered acceptable now, and vice versa. There is a great danger in confusing such trivia with real issues of standards and values, and parents who join battle with their children over these things risk forfeiting the respect that their sons and daughters feel towards their beliefs and opinions in other more important areas. The rule should be to avoid joining battle over little things, in order to avoid having to join battle over big things.

MIND TRAINING

As mentioned in Chapter 9, the claim that the education we offer to the young 'trains' the mind is very far from the truth. Most of us have little or no real control over our minds. A simple experiment can graphically demonstrate this. Put down the book for a half a minute or so, close your eyes, and stop thinking . . .

Could you do it? If so, you are very unusual. Very few people can stop the flow of thoughts for a few seconds, let alone for half a minute (and remember that repeating to yourself 'I am not thinking' doesn't count, since that is just as much a thought as any other). When I try this experiment with people, I usually follow it up with the question 'So who is in charge in there?' Who is in charge of the mind, if we cannot even stop the flow of thoughts?

And in fact it is the flow of thoughts that leads to most of our psychological problems. Anxieties, worries, impossible dreams, fear, anger, resentment, hostility, jealousy, envy and all the other things that plague the mind are sustained by the action of thought. Once we can stop the flow of thoughts, or turn the flow in the direction that leads to an experience of peace and well-being, these things are laid to rest. The mind cannot relax fully, and heal itself of psychological problems, when it is at the mercy of its own thought processes.

Mind training involves gradually schooling the mind to do what you want it to do. Not only does this allow you the relaxation and peace just mentioned, it also allows you to concentrate fully upon whatever task you happen to be doing. How often do you read the page of a book, then realize when you have done so that you didn't attend properly to a single word of it? How often do you listen to a piece of information and then find a moment later that you can't remember it, simply because you weren't attending properly to it in the first place? How often do you put something down, then realize shortly afterwards that you can't recall where you put it, simply because your mind was elsewhere when you did so? How often do you feel angry and annoyed with yourself because you seem so forgetful, scatter-brained and absent-minded?

Thinking is a wonderfully powerful and useful tool. The problem lies not with thinking, but with the inefficient and ineffective way in which we use our thinking, allowing it to intrude when it is not wanted, to take its own course instead of the one we choose, and to be discursive, fragmentary and unruly. In the East, the symbol of the mind is a monkey, because monkey-like the mind delights in distracting and unproductive chatter.

The solution is to train the mind so that it is a servant and not a master, and to gain in doing so enormous benefits in terms of efficiency, inner peace, energy (incessant, undisciplined thinking can often tire us much more than physical effort), memory and concentration.

Is this training simple, and is it suitable for our children as well as for ourselves? The answer to both parts of this question is yes, although the first yes has to be qualified by saying that something that is simple is not necessarily easy! There is a difference between the two terms, and the difference is an important one.

But first for the simple part. The essential feature in all systems of mind training is that the mind be given a stimulus of some kind upon which to focus, something upon which to concentrate, and that gently but firmly it should be required to rest upon this stimulus. The stimulus can be any one of a number of things. It can be visual (a picture, provided it is not too complicated and distracting, a geometrical design, a colour, a candle flame) or auditory (the repetition of the same sound softly and over and over again), or it can be some aspect of the body (the sensation of breathing, either at the nostrils or at the rise and fall of the abdomen, or the point just above and between the eyes). Whatever the stimulus, the mind must not be allowed to wander away from it. Each time it attempts to do so, it must be brought patiently back again.

With children, best results are obtained if the stimulus has sufficient initial interest to capture and hold the attention. A favourite picture is a good possibility, as is the light of a small bedside lamp, or an interesting pattern of some kind. The child is invited to play a mind game that consists of seeing how long he or she can look at the stimulus without letting the thoughts wander. That's all. The game can be played for a few minutes a day from around the fifth year of life onwards, preferably after listening to a bed-time story, when it is usually welcomed if for no other reason than that it serves to postpone the moment when the light is put out and the child has to settle to sleep. Children usually take to the game readily enough, and soon show themselves to be surprisingly good at it. It needn't be played every night, and should never be prolonged until interest is lost, but as the child learns it at the same time that he or she is in the process of mastering the use of language and of thought (almost all thinking is done in the form of language), it quickly becomes part of the psychological repertoire associated with these skills. Indeed probably at no other time in life is learning of this kind so easy to acquire.

As a variation, the child can be asked to raise a hand each time a thought enters the mind and lower it once the thought goes away again, and although there is no way of checking the accuracy of these signals, they can be a useful aid in the development of concentration. The game can also be played after the child has said his or her evening prayers, and here the stimulus can be a single world like 'love' or 'God', and the child invited to focus on something associated with these words, whether it be a person or an imaginary picture, or even just a good feeling.

Once children have got the idea of the game, they can be encouraged to use it as a way of relaxing the mind for sleep. Older children can use it as a way of clearing the mind of other thoughts before beginning to study, and as a way of calming themselves when upset. The game – or *meditation* to give it its proper name – is quite literally the single most effective way of training (programming if you prefer) the mind to experience its real, primal condition, untroubled by the ceaseless stream of concerns that thoughts introduce into it. A useful analogy is that of a lake. When the water of the lake is agitated it becomes muddy and opaque, but as soon as it is allowed to be still the sediment settles down and the water returns to its natural condition of clarity.

The experience of this clarity within the mind, even if only for a few minutes each day, soon begins to influence the mind even at other times. The mind concentrates better on the job in hand, is calmer and more peaceful, and the spirits generally are brighter and freer. It has immediate access to relaxation and tranquillity, and finds it easier to turn away from distracting thoughts and to deal with negative emotions such as anger and anxiety.

The subject of meditation is a fascinating one in its own right, since in a very real sense it is the study of the mind itself. Once one learns not to be set off on a wild goose chase of associations by each thought that comes into the head, one can decide to watch the arising and passing away of each thought, and notice the habits of thinking into which the mind has fallen over the years. One thought leads to another leads to another, and one can see for example how the mind churns endlessly round and round a problem of some kind without really addressing itself to a solution, or dwells endlessly on a slight or feelings of guilt or on an embarrassment of some kind, or on what might have been or on what one fantasizes might just possibly come to pass. Watching the mind in this way is a wonderful path to self-knowledge, and an invaluable aid to breaking out of old patterns of useless, time-wasting mental activity. Frequently people say to me that their minds are so busy they can't possibly learn to meditate. My answer is that it is precisely *because* our minds are so busy that we need to master the technique.

There is probably no substitute for starting young. In Tibet children were admitted into the monastery as early as 5 years old, and commenced the first stages of mind training soon afterwards. We quite literally have nothing in the West to compare with the intimate knowledge of – and control over – the mind acquired by the lamas and sages of the East. But there is no reason why we shouldn't introduce our children and ourselves to the simple forms of meditation through which this knowledge and control are acquired, and every reason why we should. (For a more detailed examination of the principles and practices of meditation see the author's *The Elements of Meditation* and *The Meditator's Handbook*, both published by Element Books.)

Conclusion

Our children are wonderful companions along a major stretch of the highway we travel through life. They variously bring joy, excitement, laughter, new interests, love and friendship, and although they can also bring their quota of frustrations and anxieties as well, these are a small price to pay for the manifold gifts they bestow upon us. Children are also great teachers. Their fresh, spontaneous way of looking at life can prompt us to start using our own eyes and ears once more, while their enthusiasm for the simple pleasures that life brings can gladden our hearts. Their openness to experience, to ideas, and to the wonder and mysteries of life can remind us of what a magical place the world is, and of how much remains to be learned of its secrets, while their intuitive spiritual awareness can inspire us on our own spiritual journey.

Children are also sensitive mirrors of our own levels of consciousness. They reflect back at us our own ways of being and our own states of mind. When children are surrounded by warm, loving people, and by the kind of physical and emotional environment that such people create, their own natures flow with the same life-enhancing qualities. When by contrast they are surrounded by anger and misunderstandings, and by an atmosphere of tension, blame and guilt, they become in their own turn awkward and difficult, and prone to a range of behavioural and personality problems. Truly if we want to know how successful we are in our own psychological lives, we need only look at and learn from our children.

Similarly, our children reflect back at us our real feelings about them. If we regard our children as awkward nuisances, or as inconveniences or as slow learners, we go part way towards making them all of these things. The manner in which we react towards our children determines in large measure the way in which they react towards the world. Call a child stupid often enough and he or she will become stupid. By contrast, show children that they are loved, cherished and thought well of, and the positive qualities implied by these adult behaviours will not be slow to emerge. Dominate a child, and he or she will either grow up cowed and with little self-confidence and initiative, or believing that domination and power are the only way to handle relationships. Treat children with democracy, and show them that their opinions and feelings are valued and respected, and they will grow up valuing and respecting the opinions and feelings of others.

Most parents protest that they love their children, so if the latter develop problems, they can't understand the reason. All too often this reason lies in the fact that the parents have never really demonstrated this love, sometimes because the love is mixed up with selfishness and possessiveness. We want our children to be the people *we* think they should be, and not the people they really are, or we want them always to satisfy our own emotional needs rather than their own, or we want them to boost our ego by making us proud in front of our friends. Sometimes it is because we don't act out our love. We are afraid of doing the wrong thing, of spoiling our children, of being too indulgent with them. Sometimes it is because our lives are so busy that we really can't find time for our children, or because other concerns and anxieties crowd our children out. Sometimes it is because we are afraid of showing our deeper and warmer feelings, having perhaps ourselves been brought up to keep them hidden. Sometimes it is because we give way too easily to impatience and annoyance, and have never learned how to come to terms with our own emotional life.

Whatever the details, they have prevented us from seeing our children as real, independent human beings, and not as extensions of ourselves or as material to be shaped in our hands, or as rather noisy and inconvenient house guests. Childhood is over all too quickly. Only when it is too late do many parents realize that they have ignored much of it, or failed to enjoy it in the way that they should. But no amount of regrets and no amount of wishing can ever bring childhood back. The childhood years are the foundation of our lives. It is during these years that others decide for us what course our lives are likely to take, and the degree of inner happiness or suffering that these lives are going to bring. Parenthood is indeed the most sacred of all trusts, and also the most fulfilling and rewarding. We are only human and cannot get every part of it right. Although it is the most important job we are ever likely to undertake, we receive no training for it, and precious little support and guidance along the way. However, the knowledge we need to help us is available, and as much of it as possible has been covered in this book.

In the final analysis, parenting is about doing our part in handing down the best to our children and avoiding the worst. As parents we are links in the chain that goes back to the first men and women in the mists of pre-history. In their own turn our children will one day become parents and play their own part in this chain, and if we have done our job well, we will make it all the easier for them to play this part successfully. It is not over-stating the case to say that the future of the human race literally depends upon the standard of parenting. If we hand on to our children qualities of love, understanding, peace and compassion, the world will survive. If we also hand on qualities of happiness and joy it will become an even better place. The choice on whether to do so or not lies with us, but we only have the very few years when our children are young in which to make it. And that doesn't give us very much time.

Further Reading

The field of child psychology is a very extensive one, and the following is only a very small selection of the books currently available. However, for readers wishing to continue their reading and to learn more about psychology, they provide a good place to start.

The best introduction to the whole field of psychology (highly readable but only for the serious student) is the mammoth *Introduction to Psychology* (11th Edition) by Rita and Richard Atkinson, Edward Smith and Daryl Bem. A much shorter introduction is *Psychology and You*, by Julia Berryman, David Hargreaves, Kevin Howells and Clive Hollin.

For those wishing to concentrate only upon childhood, *Child Development and Personality* (7th Edition) by Paul Mussen, John Conger, Jerome Kagan and Alethea Huston is excellent, as is *The Developing Child* (5th Edition) by Helen Bee.

Books specifically concerned with child rearing are the present author's *Your Growing Child: From Birth to Adolescence*, and *Baby and Child* and the various other books by Penelope Leach. A good short introduction to ways of helping your child's intellectual development is *Mind Skills* by David Lewis.

Useful Addresses

Addresses of relevance to the parent include the following:

National Childbirth Trust,
9 Queensborough Terrace, London W2 3TB.

National Children's Bureau,
8 Wakley Street, London EC1V 7QE.

National Council for One Parent Families,
255 Kentish Town Road, London NW5 2LX.

Pre-School Playgroups Association,
Alford House, Aveline Street, London SE11 5DH.

Health Education Authority,
78 New Oxford Street, London WC1A 1AH.

National Association for Maternal and Child Welfare,
First Floor, 40–42 Osnaburgh Street, London NW1 3ND.

National Association for the Welfare of Children in Hospital,
7 Exton Street, London SE1 8VE.

Child Welfare League of America,
440 First Street, NW Washington DC, 2001, USA.

International Childbirth Education Association,
PO Box 20048, Minneapolis, Minnesota, 55420 0048 USA.

International Childbirth Education Association,
PO Box 36, Westmead, 2145 New South Wales, Australia.

National Children's Bureau of Australia,
PO Box 686, Mulgrave North, Victoria 3170, Australia.

Index

adolescence 41–2, 44–5
adoptive parents 65–6
appearance 143–4
archetypes 26–7, 122
arts 80–3
autonomy 33–4, 49

bonding 48

competence 35–8, 49
co-operation 53–4
corporal punishment 59–60
creativity 80–5

discipline 57–61
dreams 117–22

emotions 28–9
Eriksen, Erik 31–2
evil 98–100
exercise 142–3

Freud, Sigmund 50–1, 52, 118

ghosts 113
gifted children 87–9
gratitude 102–5

harmony, in life 29

identity 38–45
imagination 22–6, 92–3
initiative 34–5
intelligence 85–7
interests 132–3

Jung, Carl 26, 39, 74, 118, 122

law of natural consequences 58–9, 99
learning difficulties 89–90
Lodge, Sir Oliver 68–9
love 48–50

magic 21–2, 115–17
mind training 135, 144–7
morality 36–8, 46

nature 2–4, 9, 29–30, 72

parenthood, responsibility of 4–5
poltergeists 114–15
posture 139–41
pregnancy 5–8
psychic abilities 110–13

reading 25–6, 27, 126–9
relationships, between child and siblings 14–17, 54
  between parents 9–14
  between parents and child 11–12, 27, 53–4, 56, 57, 136–7
religion 91–2
rhythm, in life 29
ritual 4, 6–8, 9

Schmeidler, Gertrude 109–10
school, starting 123–5
school refusal 133–5
science 67–75
self-assertion 100–2
self-control 46–8
self-esteem 5, 35–6, 40–1, 49, 90
sex 50–3
single parents 61–4
Socrates 76, 77
spirituality 13, 24, 43–5, 92–4
step-parents 64–5
Stevenson, Ian 110–11, 112
symbolism 3, 26–7, 95–6, 118–19

teaching 75–8, 125–9
temperament 55–7
touch 18, 138–9
trust 32–3, 48, 49

visual stimulation 17–18

Wordsworth, William 1, 19, 21